D1071135

ON THE SOURCES OF PATRIARCHAL RAGE

THE HISTORY OF EMOTIONS SERIES

EDITED BY

Peter N. Stearns, Carnegie-Mellon University
Jan Lewis, Rutgers University-Newark

On the Sources of Patriarchal Rage

The Commonplace Books of William Byrd and Thomas Jefferson and the Gendering of Power in the Eighteenth Century

KENNETH A. LOCKRIDGE

NEW YORK UNIVERSITY PRESS
NEW YORK AND LONDON

NEW YORK UNIVERSITY PRESS
New York and London

Library of Congress Cataloging-in-Publication Data
Lockridge, Kenneth A.
On the sources of patriarchal rage : the commonplace books of William Byrd and Thomas Jefferson and the gendering of power in the Eighteenth Century / Kenneth A. Lockridge.
p. cm. — (The History of Emotions series)
Includes bibliographical references and index.
ISBN 0-8147-5069-9
1. Jefferson, Thomas 1743–1826—Views on women. 2. Byrd, William, 1674–1744—Views on women. 3. Commonplace-books—History and criticism. 4. Women—History—18th century. 5. Misogyny—History—18th century. I. Title. II. Series.
E332.2.L63 1992
305.42'0973'09033—dc20 92-25809
CIP

New York University Press books are printed on acid-free paper, and their binding materials are chosen for strength and durability.

Manufactured in the United States of America

c 10 9 8 7 6 5 4 3 2 1

CONTENTS

ILLUSTRATIONS

All illustrations appear as a group following p. 74

INTRODUCTION

THIS is an essay into which I was drawn by an encounter with a commonplace book written by William Byrd II of Virginia, a man who was born in 1674 and died in 1744. So caustic was its view of women in general—as assembled in a series of paraphrased quotations and anecdotes—and in one brief outburst so intensely misogynistic, that, if the record is correct, Byrd himself felt obliged to explain his assemblage as best he could. The emotions which by his own indirect admission danced beneath the witty surface of his misogynistic commonplace entries—fear, frustration, and above all rage—entranced me. There really was, then, an age in which men's fears of and frustrations with women could be extended to nightmare proportions by assembling misogynistic fragments from the western cultural memory, from among the millions of fragments then in print, and the whole tinged with deadly rage.

For a long time I looked at other seventeenth- and eighteenth-century commonplace books, at the Bodleian Library, at the American Antiquarian Society, at the Huntington Library, at the University of Virginia's Alderman Library, and I found no other such private outbursts. But someone, Jack McLaughlin, had already found one for me and the keeper of this new commonplace book was Thomas Jefferson. Now, I had not only a fuller range of patriarchal emotions toward women to consider, emotions culminating in rage in this case as well, but also a peculiar problem. Was it significant that out of all the commonplace books I had seen it was only William Byrd and Thomas Jefferson, the two great mythmakers of the Virginia gentry, who violated the conventions of the commonplace genre by assembling such tirades?

What follows is in one respect the story of the uncovering of these men's private emotions toward women as embodied in the assemblages of culture each made, at a specific moment in time, in his commonplace book. We shall see that these assemblages had a prior history and that each was in a sense a confessional relating to events in each man's life. Primarily a close textual analysis, as it progresses however this essay also becomes more and more a reflection on the sources of patriarchal rage in these cases and in general, and on the history of the larger, more diffuse emotional and cultural category we know as misogyny. But it is not encyclopedic; it is not an essay on "The Male Creed" to rival William Byrd's own in "The Female Creed." There are whole literatures, for example, on both patriarchy and the state and on misogyny, in sixteenth- and seventeenth-century Europe and likewise on the same subjects in England. These are drawn upon as needed but referred to largely in the footnotes. For what concerns me here is the way the sources I have encountered fit into the histories of private patriarchal rage and public and private misogyny from the beginning of the eighteenth century to the early nineteenth century. Even within this rubric, what I offer is close to the sources and a very personal reflection. Someone who likes it refers to it as a slice of chocolate cake, filling but not very big. I hope others will find some quality in it but truly, not only is it not as richly developed as a European historian could make it, but it is in no sense the entire cake. I leave that to better bakers than I.

To shift metaphors, this essay is one American historian's step into and toward the wealth of understanding with which early modern European history draws us out of our ancient insularities, and into a world of shared conditions and common concerns. Foremost among those concerns is the topic of gender relations and the gendering of power and cosmology in the early modern era. Even though this present example is really masculine history and not true gender history, the fact remains that gender history in the American and European fields has both de-ghettoized "women's history" and opened up immense new avenues for those of us who study social relations, authority, and power in this period. I would be remiss if I did not thank those who have drawn me into this enterprise. Foremost among them are my friends, teachers, and occasional students (which is how my department thinks of them) Susan Juster, Jan Lewis, Jill Lepore, and Nancy Rosenberg. Thank you, all of you. Subsequently Anna Foa, Pete Becker, Peter Stearns, and Colin Jones have helped in manifold ways to make this essay a book. Julie Routson has made it a book, with her great skill and wisdom as both word processor and reader/editor.

ON THE SOURCES OF PATRIARCHAL RAGE

CHAPTER I

COMMONPLACES I: WILLIAM BYRD

COMMONPLACE books are books in which the owner has paraphrased or transcribed anecdotes, quotations, and information from other sources, usually printed. They may contain commentaries, original compositions, or even personal memos and accounts, but they are dominated by the reproduction of passages from other works. The genre originates in the classical notion that one should memorize *topoi*, or places, past utterances in which telling rhetoric and moral knowledge were inseparably embodied. When memorized, *topoi* became literally places in the mind which could serve as weapons in future rhetorical struggles. Early in the sixteenth century Erasmus revived this tradition. Literacy and print culture were then widely available, so he urged young men to write down, perhaps as an aid to memory, such *topoi* or places as they encountered in their readings. To make the task easier, he reproduced thousands of classical apothegms in several printed collections. His emphasis was less on future rhetorical battles than on the acquisition of moral knowledge, but social positioning was still implied. Thus was born the modern commonplace book which, with its infinite subgenres and combinations of these, became a common instrument of self-fashioning from the sixteenth to the twentieth centuries.[1]

Commonplace books may be the visible reproduction of linguistic memory as it in fact functions. Patterns and forms of language are quite possibly known in the mind not as a set of consistent and alternative rhetorical patterns but rather as a hodgepodge of brief examples of different linguistic genres read or overheard at different times, then adapted and assembled into more or less consistent passages in oral or written composition. So the ancients and Erasmus in turn possibly were cognitively astute when they urged that young gentry stuff their heads almost randomly with *topoi* in varying and not always elevated rhetorical genres in order to acquire the range and facility in rhetoric that life required of public persons. If the mind *is* a grab bag of bits and pieces of different linguistic genres, better to stuff it full of random examples, then, without much attention to the logic of the different genres. The ancients, and Erasmus, may have been good cognitive psychologists in another sense as well, namely in their perception that moral knowledge is inseparable from its syntax. Current theories tell us that there is no abstract moral knowledge; it exists only as embodied in particular rhetorical contexts. Morality is its syntax. Thus, for an ancient genre, the commonplace embodies a curiously modern linguistics and a post-modern sensibility.[2]

The commonplace books Erasmus inspired are post-modern in another sense as well, for they are not reproductions of culture as ideology so much as moment-to-moment assemblages or enactments of culture, performed from out of the grab bag of bits and pieces which any culture makes available. They are the ultimate in *bricolage*. It follows from this—if anything, in a post-modern age, follows from anything—that, while each commonplace book is an effort to assemble culture out of scrap-like bits toward a synthesis of standard moral and social knowledge, each is also unique. Each enactor of culture, each keeper of a commonplace, is unique; each occasion of enactment, each set of entries, is adapted to a unique moment in the enactor's life. This is culture as cultural anthropologists have come to understand it.[3]

For it is important to realize in all of this, that the author of a commonplace has a universe of literally hundreds of thousands of anecdotes and passages to draw upon, and that each book enacts out of this pool an assemblage of *at most* several thousand pieces in a life-time, perhaps a thousand a decade, a hundred or so in a year, or a few dozen in a month or so. These are transient, personal, momentary assemblages. They *seem* universal, standardized, boring, because they embody a universal theory of cognition and a theory that cultural knowledge is to be found in certain albeit broadly encompassing sets of printed sources. But within this broad theoretical uniformity they are, or can be, highly selective, and they are therefore powerfully unique and personal assemblages at the intersections differing individuals made with the standard knowledges of their times. A commonplace is an event or series of events in a life, not a mere collection.

We do not yet know exactly how, in the "normal case," if there can be said to be such a thing in a genre so varied and individually selective, the keeper of a commonplace used this instrument in the fashioning of a self. So little has been written on commonplaces that neither individual studies nor theory yet exists. Commonplaces were one among several books of the self which many gentlemen kept, customary components, along with diaries and letterbooks, in an inner library by which identity was shaped through memory and writing. Such instruments of identity were posterior to the social intercourse by which genteel identity was initially shaped, in coffee houses and drawing rooms, in public and domestic spaces. Of all such books of the self, commonplaces were superficially the least reflective of what had happened in the prior world of social intercourse. That is, diaries and letters explicitly remembered and re-shaped previous social discourse and projected it into the future in permanent form; they were obvious instruments of the reshaping of a previously enacted public identity in a private or semi-private forum. On the surface commonplaces "remembered" almost arbitrarily only a few pieces of a more formal cultural memory which had already been consigned to public print and encountered in this form. Yet commonplace books are like diaries and letters in that in all three cases the self is being defined privately for a fictionalized audience (and in the case of letters also for a real audience) in terms of its relationship to a selection of prior events and knowledge. If diaries and letters defined a fictionalized self in relation to prior encounters with personally known individuals, then commonplaces helped define a fictionalized self in relation to the utterances of unmet others which had somehow gained the status of print. Further, commonplace books were fully as selective as diaries and letters; indeed more so, as in this case the individual was selecting prior events to interact with from a vastly larger field than mere personal experience. Beneath their surface sheen of public knowledge, then, these are profoundly instruments of personal identity.

This much we can know. And we know that, for men and women with claims to gentility, whose verse, plays, and essays if they wrote such at all did not enter the public realm, let alone the canonical literature, diaries, letters, and commonplaces were probably the chief written instruments of what Stephen Greenblatt has called "Renaissance self-fashioning."[4] But exactly how all such private writings, and specifically commonplaces, entered into the process of identity formation whose more public and canonical aspects Greenblatt describes, and exactly what theories of identity, culture, and the state such private self-fashionings implied, are issues vastly open to contest.

One initial approach to commonplaces and to their role at the intersection of print culture, personal identity, and the Renaissance social order, it seems to me, is to consider those occasions on which commonplaces were most obviously instruments of personal identity and even of personal self-justification, occasions on which there can be no doubt that a crisis of the subject is working itself out through the medium of entering bits of print culture into a commonplace book. Let me emphasize that such occasions may not relate to the "normal case" at all, and so may tell us little about the "normal" uses of commonplaces. For on such occasions the authors reveal their personal engagement by breaking one of the cardinal rules of all commonplaces in all times and places: they go on and on at great length, almost obsessively, about a single, emotionally laden subject. This breaks the rules of variety, change, and general detachment implicit in both Erasmus's and Locke's advice on keeping a commonplace, rules which I have found to prevail overwhelmingly in the scores of seventeenth- and eighteenth-century commonplace books I have read.[5] The passages in question may fairly be labelled "outbursts" or "tirades" with respect to their violation of these central rules of the genre. Such passages, I would suggest, enable us to get some initial substantive use out of the genre. Moreover, they may represent not so much a violation of the genre—though they do violate one of its major rules—as a heightening and focussing of the ways in which personality, print culture, selectivity, occasion, and era *always* combined, albeit ordinarily less obsessively so, to make commonplaces expressive of the enactment of culture and the shaping of identity in pre-revolutionary western society.

It is in this sense that I wish to discuss two particular commonplace books. These books are witnesses to the events in which two men, both Virginia gentlemen of the eighteenth century, assembled their culture—literally enacted or embodied it in these books of themselves—on the issue of gender. The books are in the same sense and simultaneously confessionals. They are confessionals of intense personal crises of gender relations. What I have found in these confessional enactments on gender disturbs me, though it does not surprise me. It is reminiscent of Foucault yet more evocative of some lines of feminist theory, and in its specificity and implications it may embody that theory in particularly significant ways.[6]

Let us look together at a long set of passages found toward the end of an unpublished commonplace book by William Byrd II. Byrd was a Virginia planter, slaveowner, and politician active in the first decades of the eighteenth century. He kept this book while he was in London circa 1721–1726. He was then forty-seven to fifty-two years old. His is an Erasmian commonplace whose paraphrased anecdotes have from the beginning been obsessively concentrated on a wittily scathing view of women, on political power, on political failure, and on the effort to achieve philosophical resignation in the face of failed ambition.[7] It is essentially a book in which the self is being redrawn to a lesser scale. Now, around 1725 or 1726, two-thirds of the way through its length, it suddenly departs from its gradual movement toward a philosophical acceptance of failure. . . .

An initial sequence of eight entries serves as a kind of porch or prelude to what is to follow. Byrd has been entering anecdotes on one of his favorite subjects, the game of office-seeking and its attendant political corruption—a game at which, incidentally, he himself has failed miserably—when he abruptly takes up the issue of male inadequacy and insatiable female sexuality. There is nothing in itself unusual in this mixture of themes, as politics and gender have been blended together in brief prior sequences in this commonplace, always with an implied subtext of male/Byrd's failure, but this time he departs farther and longer into female sexuality than ever before.

> T'is a Common thing for Rams to tup 50 or 60 Sheep in one night which denotes a prodigious natural Vigor especially when we consider that they Seldome miss to impregnate the Female every leap they make. how short do poor men fall of these Feats![8]

The mirror image of male inadequacy is of course female lasciviousness, which in the ensuing entry is placed in conflict with women's reproductive duties, and is therefore a lust which must be kept under strict patriarchal control.

Women are most lascivious about the time their Terms begin to flow, because of the irritation which the flux of blood & Spirits gives their **Parts** at that time: But Moses was very wise in forbiding copulation under that circumstance, because tho' the Inconvenience may be very little to the Partys themselves *besides the Impurity* yet if a child shoud be got at that time it woud be a miserable Weakling, that woud be hardly worth the trouble of bringing up, & tis odds but it woud come dead into *ye* world.

Byrd then enters the observation that even "the natives of Brasile" are careful to prohibit sexual activity on the part of females who have conceived because their blood, rushing to the womb on subsequent copulations, might otherwise create a dangerous second conception, threatening to the success of the first and to the life of the prospective mother. Uncontrolled female lust, blood, and reproductive power can combine to destroy the reproductive process and women's very lives. "This piece of prudence," the entry continues, is more inviolably observed in the aboriginal societies of the Americas than in "the politer parts of the world where pleasure and Luxury have got entirely the better [of men]."

Without a pause, the next entry seems to suggest that to the contrary, in "politer parts" some men are willing to indulge in self-mutilation to keep pace with female desire.

A certain great Performer with the Sex finding his vigour begin to abate was so unwilling to part with any part of that dear Pleasure, that he causd one of his Legs to be cut off, that so the bloud & Spirits which usd to nourish that Limb, might add strength to those which remaind, and increase his abilitys with the allureing Sex.

So uncontrollable is female lust, indeed, that women can suppress it only by drinking the blood of the object of their desire, or by annihilating him.

Faustina the Daughter of Antoninus Pius was desperately in Love with a Gladiator. She was sensible of the absurdity of so low a passion, & tryd all the Remedys of Prudence as well as abstinence against it. But alas all her Endeavours were vain, & had the effect that oil woud have towards extinquishing a flame. At length she consulted the oracle which told her, nothing woud calm her concupiscence but drinking the bloud of her Beloved. This she did, & afterwards hated him to that degree that she causd him to be put to death. A very cruel Remedy against Love invented *to be sure* by the Devil himself.

Apparently the only way to control that desire which destroys both reproduction and men, and to turn women into successful bearers of children, is for men to enter them from behind, with women in a submissive posture.

Luxury has taught men to caress their wives before: but Nature woud rather teach them to caress them behind. Indeed When he attacks her before he has more pleasure, because the Lips of the Persons engag'd & several other parts of their bodys meet in this Posture, which dont in the other, & the Penetration is commonly more home. But tis however agreed by all anatomists, that the Womb of a Woman is better situated for conception, when she rests upon her hands & Knees, than when she lyes upon her Back. For in that Posture the Bottom of the womb lys lower much than the Orifice, & consequently the Seed may more easily be injected into it. Besides if a Woman expects a Husband shoud perform Duty after she's with child, twill be much safer for her to receive him behind, because the Violence of the Shock will not be so dangerous upon her Buttocks, as upon her Belly, where the tender Fruit lys reposited.

Twas the advice of a man very knowing in the nature of mankind, when a Lady enquird of him what courses she had best take to be prolifick. Eat fish madam, said he, drink Water, & f--- upon all four. She took his advice & had a child after she was **Fourty**.

The commonplace then returns to its usual mixture of anecdote and witty repartée, pausing two entries later only to recall that it is always incumbent upon the man to wear the breeches in his marriage.

A man & his Wife were one morning in high dispute which shoud wear the Breeches. In the midst of the Fray somebody knockt at the Door, & wanted to speak with the Master of the house. Pray friend said the good man, tarry a moment, til that matter is decided & you shall have an answer. Then he returnd to the charge, & haveing subdued His Spouse with . . . arguments that convinced her *only* of his superiority, he went back to *ye* Stranger, & gave him audience to his satisfaction.

This unusually prolonged series of entries has introduced themes which will soon be taken up at still greater length and depth. Briefly, for the next three pages and twenty-odd entries the commonplace resumes its usual repartée with tales of men and sometimes women in all walks of life, tales full of wisdom as well as wit, and in which all aspects of life come under scrutiny. Insofar as women appear in conflict with men in some of these tales, the battle of wits between them is very evenly drawn. But gradually the entries drift back to topics which may have been very much on the writer's mind, to old age, to virginity, and to "a fashionable distemper" that left a man "wasted to a cinder."

It is at this point that the true outburst begins. The writer enters a tale in which a philosopher, the very term he is now using to style himself, observes that sex is not just a pastime, but that it evokes death and life as well, and notes that through sexual intercourse lies man's only path to immortality.

It was the hard Fate of a grave Philosopher to fall in love with a Damsel, with whome he desird to have an affair; He determind to put it to Her, but instead of makeing love in the language of other Mortals, when he got the girle alone, come my Dear said he, let you & I go this moment and make our Selves immortal; & since we must dye ourselves let us get a child that may represent us, & he another and so into all generations. This is the only way left for Man to live for ever in this world, & that way let us resolve to take.

This single entry seems to have opened vast conjunctions to Byrd's mind. Over the next few hours or days or weeks—it is not certain what time was involved—he appears to have ransacked his memory and formidable library for related quotations, as the next seven pages and thirty-five entries surge down the mental avenues opened by the thought, implicit in this passage, that even philosophers need to have intercourse with women in order to become immortal. These thirty-five entries represent a set of appropriated and implicitly linked reflections on male and female sexual anatomy, sexuality, and reproductive power which extends far longer than any other set of entries on any subject or set of linked subjects in the entire book. The second entry in this series sets the tone for what follows. They have us by the balls, it seems to be saying: "A Poor Woman was indicted of Treason, for offering to take Charles the 9th of France by the privy Parts."

The woman who had Charles IX by the balls leads to the question of male sexual adequacy. Perhaps the writer was reassured to know that: "There are many instances of Men who have 3 testicles, & some have only one, & others again have none that ever appear out of their Belly, and yet all these have begot Children. An Instance of those who have had 3, was Agathocles King of Sicily; & an Instance of those whose Testacles have not descended out of their Belly, was Monsieur Argentan, which hinderd not their Wives *at least* from haveing children."

Even with one testicle, then, the other presumably removed by a woman like the one who offered such *lèse majesté* to Charles IX, men are still strong enough to reproduce. On the other hand, as the next entry suggests, under the "one-sex model" of human sexual anatomy prevailing at the time, a woman's sexual parts are very like a man's, so women are no weaklings either: "The Clitoris in a woman is in many things like a mans Penis, it has a nut & prepuse like that, & swells very much in the act & desire of copulation; however it is not perforated, but is the *Supream* seat of pleasure in the exercises of love."

When you think about it, in fact, even a moderate clitoris can be as large as an old man's penis; thus, the next entry: "Tis said the Privitys of man grow less and dwindle away by excessive abstinence, of which *St* Martin is reported to be a remarquable Instance, who observd such strict Rules of abstinence, & exercisd such Austeritys upon himself, that when the women came to lay him out after he was dead, they coud hardly find out any Penis at all, *at most not larger than a moderate Clitoris*. So that the Fair are not much out of the way, when they choose a Lover by his stomach."

Indeed, a reproductively weak man may in turn leave his sons shortchanged as well: "In the formation of a male child, if there be any Superfluity of the generative matter, it is thrown in to the Penis, to make that larger than the common proportion; and if the same matter happen to fall short, the poor Penis must suffer for it by being less than the ordinary standard. But in the case of a Female child, this defect or abundance go's all into their **Feet**, & the Parts to which they bear the greatest proportion."

Is it also possible that philosophers, being men of large understanding, have small penises, which makes it difficult for them to achieve immortality? Certainly the converse is true. Monstrously equipped men, though weak in the head, will surely reproduce, if they don't kill the woman in the process: "Tis a standing observation, that men on whome nature has bestowd the largest Privitys, have the least understanding. The longer a Penis is, the surer work tis like to make in the business of Generation, because the Seed is injected with more certainty into the womb by reaching nearer to it. Except the length be monstrous, & then tis more likely to lessen the number of the liveing, rather than increase it."

Our troubled and philosophical male, the keeper of this ever more uncommon commonplace, then enters a long proposal he attributes to Plato's *Commonwealth*, but which I think belongs to Thomas More's *Utopia*.

In Plato's commonwealth it was ordaind, that in case 2 Persons had thoughts of marriage, they shoud See one another stark naked before they were betrothed, reaconing it much better for the Peace of Familys, that defects in the person shoud be discoverd before wedlock than afterwards. Tis said the Muscovites are wise enough to follow this prudent method, and are not content to see one anothers Bodys naked:

but desire also to unmask their *very* Souls too, by seeing each other very drunk, before the Engagement has gone too far; that so they may secure their Retreat, if any *discoverys* happen to be made to the disadvantage of either.

This is a proposal that men and women should see one another naked before betrothal, to discover any defects. It isn't said whether the defect in mind is a missing testicle, a small penis, or a large clitoris, but there follows an account of a custom in Muscovy that souls as well as bodies should be bared, in drunkenness, before marriage. Is the transcriber saying that small penises may have weak souls or large clitorises overly strong ones?

The next quotation may give a clue to the answer: "T'is reported that Cornelia Mother of the Graechi, was so narrow that she *conceivd without looseing her maidenhead*, and there was work for the Surgeon before any thing coud be done by the midwife." Further: "Some women in childbed have so bad a time of it, that both overtures burst into one, and then Nature is so kind in the healing *of* the Breach, that the Entrance into Joy is much narrower then it was before." So women hardly need a penis to conceive, or possibly not much penetration, a theme which is to recur in short order, and they heal after childbirth as if nothing had happened. Women are strong characters indeed, possessing an anatomical strength which borders on strength of soul. Which is on the other hand fortunate for men with small parts, as women can do the job in spite of little penises!

Penile size is not the only problem men encounter in the face of formidable female sexual anatomy and reproductive powers. Failure to obtain erection is another, though there may be a remedy: "To rub the Penis with oyl of Lavender is of great use to procure Erection: but the drink usd in Provence calld Sambajeu, is much better for that purpose; which is compounded of Wine, yolk of Eggs, Saffran, Sugar, & mace, which may be boild together, or else drunk raw with glorious Success."

A recipe for stopping the flow of blood follows, not explicitly sexual but a subject to which this morcellated and borrowed commonplace narrative will return in time and then unmistakably in the context of female reproductive power. What we proceed to instead is, once again, a female sexual and reproductive anatomy which in one way or another is too much for males. Remedies are suggested if women are too large: "A Decoction of what the French call grande consoude, is the best wash a lady of large naturall Parts can use to make them less. Steel medicines are also good for this purpose."

On the other hand the woman may be too tight, a problem for which we are offered another recipe. True, "straight" vaginas are likely to have maidenheads, as well, and so be pure. But Tiberius obviously found even virgins threatening, or perhaps he thought he was doing them a favor: "The Romans of old erected a Statue in honour of Virginity. This Statue was calld Bucea Veritatis, & stood erect upon a Pedistal with its mouth open. If any Virgin was Suspected of haveing lost her Maidenhead she might claim the priviledge of justifying her Innocence by puting her finger into the Statues mouth, & if she drew it out whole, she was a woman of honour: but if she had been poluted her Finger was in danger of being bit off. By an Edict publisht by Tiberius no Virgin cou'd be executed for any crime til the Hangman had first deflowerd her, which was a cruel complement paid to Virginity." In Africa, on the other hand, a virgin is scarcely better off. Stitched up to ensure her virginity, on her wedding night she must first suffer the stitches being "rip't out again." Counting the monstrous penis of an earlier entry, this African tale is the third example of sexual violence inflicted on women in the first fourteen anecdotes on male and female sexuality.

The train of thought then jumps from punishing virginity back again to female reproductive power. "Some women have been got with Child without looseing their maidenhead, when neither the Hymen nor nymphae have been in the least torn or injurd, so that their pregnancy has appeard Miraculous." Women can also produce milk without intercourse with men, and indeed men may become so weak and feminized that *they* suckle the babes: "Some women have had milk in their Breasts who had never had amorous Commerce with man: nay there are instances too of Men who have had milk & given Suck without the help of a Miracle. Nay Travellors tell us tis no uncommon thing in the Eastern part of Affrick for the men to have milk & help Suckle the children." Women really don't need men at all, save when men function as women!

The fact that women hardly need men for successful reproduction then recurs in the context of nursing, in a selection which implies that menstrual blood may be the real key to the autonomous reproductive or at least nursing power women possess: "Some naturallists are of opinion, that any young women of a healthy sanguine complection, woud have the milk come into their breasts, without haveing had any commerce with a man, if they will let a child suck them every day for a few days successively, for then their Terms will be derivd that [w]ay and changed into milk."

The cumulative picture implied is one of women sexually and reproductively stronger than men, indeed reproductively virtually independent of men. Yet somehow women demand men's sexual attentions: "The Spartans had so much Regard for Marriag[e] that they enacted a Law by which they condemnd all old Bachelors above the age of 24 to be whipt publickly by the women upon a certain Festival, and the Women were sure to lay it on very heartily, for shewing so great a disregard to their charming Sex." Is it an accident that the following entry depicts a kind of preemptive genocide in the womb? "Where there are twins of different sex tis observd that the Female Seldome lives because the Male takes from it too much the natural *nourishment* & starves it in its Mothers Belly." With this entry the contest between men and women once again assumes the dimensions of a life-or-death struggle between two similar yet profoundly different races, who in theory need one another to reproduce, though in fact women scarcely need men, and who otherwise threaten, torture, and consume one another.

Demanding women and male aggression in the womb somehow take us back to privy parts, and to the theme of adequacy in intercourse rather than in reproduction. "Good women" look out for and protect male performance in intercourse, for they "generally cut the Naval string of a boy as long as they can, & that of a Girle as Short, imagining that the Privitys of the Male will be the longer for it, & those of the Female the straiter."

Sexual adequacy continues as the theme and we pass from the Emperor Tiberius (once more) who caused "naughty" murals to be painted round his bedroom "but all these moveing Prospects coud not stir his feable constitution," to "the Lesbian Sappho," who clearly did not need men, "an inclination not altogether unknown to the Females of this Island."

Halfway through this long outburst, the two dominant themes, women's sexual anatomy and powers, and their reproductive powers, are brought together in a pair of anecdotes. In one of these both female promiscuity and near-parthenogenesis are linked as common acts of female power. But in the other female lasciviousness is accompanied by sterility, so that it appears as if women's sexual and reproductive superiorities are in truth contradictory: "Barren women are commonly more lascivious than fruitfull ones, because [of] the Heat of the womb, which is often the cause of Sterility, & at the same time the fomenter of wantoness." Hot wombs make lusty, but barren, women.

As if the preceding anecdote had satisfied him that women cannot dominate men *both* sexually *and* reproductively, the writer ends all consideration of female reproductive prowess. Women who lust cannot reproduce at all let alone without men. Does it follow that men who wish to reproduce themselves should pick women without strong sexual desires? If so, the fear entailed in this man's assembled reflections may have led him to violate the assumptions of a period in which female orgasm was considered a vital ingredient in successful reproduction.[9] Be that as it may, the second half of this long series of anecdotes focuses exclusively on the theme of female sexual desire and male sexual inadequacy, perhaps revealing the author's underlying concerns. Anatomy is no longer the focus, however; swelling clitorises and shrinking penises give way to what probably always lay beneath such tales, the threat of an insatiable female lust. Yet it is not lust alone, but cleverness as well, and in the end, in the combination of female lust and cleverness, it is a pure and deadly power that women wield over feeble men. Men's best efforts cannot avail to save themselves from this combination. Drawn to women by a desire for sex and by their need to reproduce themselves men are consumed and discarded.

Popilia being askt by a very curious Person of her own Sex, why Brutes woud never admit the male after they had once conceivd? answerd with the true Spirit of a woman, because they are Brutes, and know no better.

The Reason why a Cuckold is infamous in most Countrys, is because it is supposd to happen either by his own ill-treatment of the Wife, or at least by his own folly in Suffering her to have liberty & opportunity to abuse Him. Accordingly twas the Custome formerly in France, in case the Wife was taken in adultery, for the Magistrate to set the poor Husband upon an Ass with His Face towards the Brutes Tail, and make the naughty wife lead him thro' the Streets, and proclaim with a loud voice, **Behold I can lead these 2 asses wherever I please.**

Semiramis was very strongly inclind to the passion of Love: but at the same time so great a Prude that she constantly took care to order every Man, with whome she had an affair, to be instantly bury'd alive that he might not either thro' vanity or levity, discover her Secret. Tis pity she had not respited their punishment til they had boasted of her Favors, and then I think they woud have had their Reward. But she took it for granted all men were Traytors to the Fair & therefore woud not wait for their Treason, but orderd their punishment before hand to make sure work of it.

By this time, the writer's anecdotes are becoming longer and longer, in the end becoming the longest in the entire commonplace. Whether he is finding these entries intact in his sources or is letting anecdotes run together in a white heat of fascination is hard to tell, as in many cases his Erasmian rephrasings make it impossible to ascertain his exact source; but I suspect that he is himself assembling these extended entries from multiple sources. The issue now quickly moves onto that classic battleground of the sexes, how frequently men may, can, should, must have intercourse with women. The two longest passages are literally a battleground of multiple anecdotes across which weak men, lascivious women, puissant men, and once again lustful women joust in an exhausting tournament of love which can have but one outcome.

Man, considering how frail, how dependent, & depravd a creature he is, never makes so ill a figure, as when he is vain of his Perfections, & gives himself airs of Sufficiency. Nay rather than suffer him Self to be inconsiderable, he is vain of his follys, & *had* rather glory in his Shame, than not distinguish him Self at all. Amongst the rest of our Vanitys, there is none more ridiculous than when we make ostentation of our Exploits with the women. Whereas supposeing every word we said of our might in that particul[ar] were true, theres hardly a Brute in the Creation but is able to perform oftener with his Female than we can do. Nay a poor sparrow or even a diminutive Fly coud they Speak as well as they coud in AEsops time, might call the ablest of our Boasters a Fumbler. The Emperor Proculus pretended that he had laid with an Hundred Sarmatian Women, which he had taken in the wars, in less than a Fort'-night. Mighty Feats for an Emperour to glory in, when a Ram will tup that number of Ewes in one night & impregnate them all! Crusius tells us a Story that a strong *Dog of a* Servant in his neighbourhood, got ten wenches with child in one night. This indeed was doing business, and no man upon Record ever did more, except Hercules himself, who is famed for having begot 50 boys in one night upon the Bodys of 50 Athenian Damsels, and if this was true, it was the greatest of all his Atcheivements. The Spaniards are famous for doing handsome things with the Women as appears by the complaint of a Catalonian Lady exhibited against her Husband. She fell down at the Kings feet & implord his Protection. The good King askt her what might be her Grievanc[e] Lord Sire said she, I am a dead Woman unless your Majesty protect me from a hard hearted Husband. What dos he do to you Madam replyd the King? Alas Sire said she, he dos more to me than any Husband in all Spain dos to His Wife, He is impertinent at least ten times every [n]ight. By *St* Iago answerd the King if this be true he deserve[s] to dye, for he will make every *other* Woman in my Dominions despise her Husband. However he mitigated his punishment & made him give Security for his good behaviour, and strictly injoind him not to assault the complainant more than 6 times a night for the future.

When the ancients painted Venus, they generally shewd Mercury in some part of the Picture, which carryd this notable instruction, [t]hat we shoud always let Reason have some Share in our Love, to direct [a]nd keep it with in bounds, least what is intended by Providence for our ha [ms. torn] be abused by our folly to our distruction. And therefore Solon who was [a] wise man, & studyd the preservation of his Athenians, made a law, that no man shoud on pain of castration caress his Wife or any other woman more than 3 times in a month. This Edict raisd a terrible Mutiny amongst the Women, which made it necessary for that grave Lawgiver to indulge them with one time more, and confine them to once a week. Indeed the Jews are more liberal to the lovely Sex, and allow the men to gratify their Spouses as often as they can but twice a week they must do *it by the Law* and in case the Husband fell short in this necessary *duty*, His wife might have right done her by the magistrate. The ancient Philosophers were much in disgrace with the fair Sex, for recommending moderation *in* the pleasures of Love: but none so much as Aeas who was marryd 6 years and yet solaced his Wife no more than **thrice** the whole time. Yet this was pure continence in him, & not the least incapacity, for he Struck out a child every **Flourish** he made. Messalina, who obliged 25 men in 20 hours, and Cleopatra, who in one night stood the attacque of 105 young Fellows, woud have made sad Disciples to that Philosopher. The first of these illustrious Ladys when she had passt thro' the whole number askt if there were no more, for tho she was tired she was not satisfyd, *assata Sum Sed not ratiata*.

For those of you who, like me, are poor Latinists, the writer's concluding remark by Messalina is a garbling of line 130 from Juvenal's sixth satire, *Lassata sem sed non satiata*: I was worn out but not satiated. This is followed by an observation from Cato, to the effect that "in matters of love the only sure way to conquer is to run away," to which the writer adds his comment that this applies not only to women but also to men. What he clearly means is that women should flee before their lusts become uncontrollable while men should flee before they are consumed.

The entire outburst ends with a series of recipes for controlling male desire, by implication in order to save men from being consumed by female desire. In some earlier anecdotes, philosophers and aged and feeble men had seemed especially vulnerable to women's lust; but now it is all men who are at risk, and the problem is not so much male age or feebleness as male desire, which draws men into a contest they cannot win. A leaden girdle upon the loins, sour lemons, and abundance of cooling lettuce can be used. "Others have applied a Plaister of white Lillys to the Small of their backs and taken them inwardly to dry up their Seed, and Stiffle their disorderly Inclinations." And there it is, at last. Female desire is an invitation to disorder as well as, with Semiramis, to death. All male power and order, like life itself, dissolves in the female-dominated vortex of desire. Men must stifle their seed, their very chance to reproduce and to become immortal, in the hope of avoiding the deadly disorder of that vortex. Perhaps they must nearly stifle life itself: "A deccoction of Hemlock *moderately taken* will have the same Effect." Men can imitate Socrates and take the hemlock, half-dying in order to suppress their own feebler desires, suppressing in the process their chances of self-reproduction, in order to maintain their ordering of the world, which is their true life.

I won't reflect on this chamber of horrors. Not yet. For, as suddenly as it began, it is ended by the insertion in the manuscript of a series of love letters cut from the writer's letterbook. These letters were written to the last of a long series of elegant English ladies who had refused to marry him. This lady is identified only as "Charmante" and she had turned him down in the last months of 1722, at most three or four years before the preceding passages were inscribed in the commonplace. What was different about "Charmante," the letters show, was that the writer had disclosed himself to her by sending her an artificial but deeply revealing self-portrait which he had written some years before. He had sent her himself, and she had refused him. In fact, she had not even answered his letters.

The letters are followed in turn by a long reflection by the writer on his failure to win Charmante. He makes it clear that she was desirable but promiscuous, with "more charms than honor." She had permitted him "many a close hugg and tender squeeze," not to mention "other familiarities," and then turned him down for a younger man renowned for his wit. At this point the writer launches into a long warning on the dangers of wit, as if this were the sole criterion on which he had been rejected.[10] But surely we are entitled to ask here if, by inserting these letters at this point in the commonplace, just after his long, agonized reflection on female power, in a kind of insertion without precedent in his many books-of-himself, he is not also telling us the real source of his hostility toward women. By inserting these letters to break off his tirade against women, he seems to be saying that, in his own mind, he fears it was in fact his age, his private parts, his reproductive and sexual inadequacy, and not simply his lack of wit, which had forced him to endure this last, bitter rejection.

To understand fully what is going on here we have to leave the commonplace and go to the man. William Byrd was born in Virginia in 1674 and thereafter educated in London. He became a transatlantic gentleman, politician, and writer who lived half his life in London and half in Virginia, and who immediately after this episode settled down permanently in his inherited life as a Virginia planter and politician. He was a self-styled patriarch and man of power whose life we know very well. Before we reflect on his attitudes on female anatomy, sexuality, reproduction, and power, and on his tortured gendering of these constructs in his commonplace, we need to consider more carefully his previous history as a patriarch.

Byrd's mother had previously been married to Samuel Filmer, an early Virginia planter and son of Sir Robert Filmer, author of *Patriarcha* and the great ideologue of patriarchal justifications for the state in early seventeenth-century England. When the younger Filmer had died, in Virginia, Byrd's father, William Byrd I, had married the widow and soon addressed the elder Filmer in his letters as "father"! Despite this acquired heritage, and contrary to prevailing uses of his famous diaries, our William Byrd II wasn't very successful either with women or as a patriarch.[11] His lifelong ambition to be made Royal governor of Virginia, or at least lieutenant governor, and so to attain unequivocal status as an English gentleman of rank, led him repeatedly into inappropriate courtships of English women far above him in standing and in some cases in wealth. Already in his early years in London, from 1690 to 1705, he experienced rejections which were often crushing.

Probably led astray by his sexual passions—a weakness he chronicled in his self-portrait—he married the temperamental Lucy Parke while in Virginia in 1706. He lived with her in Virginia until early 1715. She had no real fortune to offer but her father, Daniel Parke, was one of the very few colonial-born gentlemen to be made governor of a Royal colony, namely of the Windward Islands in 1705. Acquiring that association by marriage was certainly attractive to Byrd. His diary of 1709–1712 is full of quarrels and sexual reconciliations with Lucy, a history in which, since she was often "breeding," frequently suffered miscarriages, and was thereafter ill, the inflicted desire seems to have been more his than hers.

What has not been known is that he left her. In 1711 his friend Parson Dunn abandoned his wife, herself a friend of Lucy's named Mary Jeffreys Dunn. Lucy then brought Mrs. Dunn to live in the Byrd household. What ensued is documented in a long letter Byrd wrote to a fictive friend named "Dunella." Gradually, he says, Mrs. Dunn gained ascendancy over Lucy. She and Lucy then usurped his patriarchal authority within the household, taking over total control of material resources and of the house servants, something Byrd could not bear. When the two women moved to gain control of one of the plantation's artisans, a weaver, he declared that a boundary had been crossed which must not be violated. Lucy must choose between Mrs. Dunn and himself. The letter implies that Byrd and Lucy are already sexually estranged and that separation will ensue if Mrs. Dunn's hold over Lucy is not broken.

For all his threats, however, Byrd's initial actions were curiously passive. The letter makes it clear that all his previous warnings had had no impact on either woman. The letter itself was a feeble device, left out in the hope that Mrs. Dunn would read it and repent, or that Lucy would see how near he was to leaving her and return to him and to his conception of his domestic authority. The claims in the letter notwithstanding, one wonders if he had truly confronted either woman. What he then did instead was to flee to England.

Byrd had had reason enough to go abroad already by 1711, when Mrs. Dunn arrived in his household, for by then his political and financial affairs were in a disarray which could only be righted in London. But he did not ask official permission to leave until late in 1713, by which time "Incendia" [Mrs. Dunn] had begun playing fast and loose with his domestic authority.[12] From the long history of building tensions it portrays, the "Dunella" letter was written after 1713, probably sometime in 1714. Moreover, it refers to his wife as "breeding." Since no miscarriages are recorded for Lucy in 1713 or 1714, it is possible that "breeding" refers to her pregnancy with their daughter Wilhelmina, which could have begun as early as February 1715 and which terminated in a successful delivery on November 6, 1715. If the reference was to the pregnancy with Wilhelmina, then Byrd's "Dunella" letter of complaint was written in 1715, and it was indeed a last, desperate plea for his wife to restore his authority, for it was followed immediately by his departure for England early in that year. His arrival there is not clearly documented but he was sending letters from London to friends in Virginia by the middle of 1715.[13]

William Byrd's first family was never again reunited. Lucy left their two daughters in Virginia and joined Byrd in London in 1716, where they were reconciled; but that very autumn, in the height of the social season, she caught the smallpox and died.

In 1717 Byrd was still in London, still hoping to be made governor of Virginia, and he began to pursue the young daughter of the Commissioner of the Excise. The story is long and painful, so let me just say that the courtship ended in 1718 in a rejection as utterly emasculating as an aging, colonial, would-be patriarch and gentleman could possibly experience. By his own account he broke down in tears and felt close to insanity. This crisis was followed promptly by his political neutering by a Board of Trade thoroughly fed up with his relentless prosecution of what they felt was his inappropriate political ambition to become Virginia's governor. After a short visit to Virginia to apologize for his subversive ambitions to the governor there, an English officer with a distinguished record in combat in the continent, he returned to London to find a wife, only to be rejected by at least two more well-placed young ladies, "Minionet" and, at last, "Charmante." Here our flashback ends, for here he enters the pages of his commonplace book.[14]

In sum, until this moment in time William Byrd had led a life which had seen the failure of his domestic and political ambitions, and seen multiple rejections by women whose fortunes might have turned political failure to political success. Charmante was merely the last of these women. This may be the larger message he is leaving us, by interleaving his letters to her in a text that has turned so coruscatingly hostile to women. Regardless of its exact message his personal history leaves little doubt that this assemblage of culture functions for him as a sort of confessional.

What is the structure of William Byrd's confessional tirade on women, sexuality, reproduction, and power in his commonplace book, and how does it construct gender? To say that it appears to release years of failure and frustration, much of it with women, in a burst of fury still leaves us needing to understand what mental categories are invoked on such an occasion. To agree, with Foucault, that in the eighteenth century most sexual literature is implicitly or explicitly confessional, is only to ask what exactly it is in this instance that is being so convulsively confessed.[15] Patriarchy should not be known by its worst cases only, but its worst constructions should be known, and understood. This is all the more so since, as we shall see, while outbursts such as William Byrd's are rare, there is at least one other available, an even more famous case, so a larger structure of meanings must hang suspended around them both.

The real event in Byrd's agonized soliloquy on sexuality is in important senses sub-rhetorical. While he is rephrasing and commenting upon the thirty-five anecdotes and "facts" on sexuality that he enters here, digesting them to a degree into a rhetoric that is in a significant degree his own, the real action is the implicit linking going on beneath this half-borrowed, half-digested rhetorical surface. From anecdote to anecdote in Byrd's mind a process is taking place which can only be likened to free association. To coin a metaphor, the mental grammar of sexuality is implicit in the process of linking together these entries. More important than the utterances are the spaces between them, containing much of Byrd's implicit construction of gender. A routine unpacking of "his" surface rhetoric is simply not a reliable way to proceed.

Text and subtext taken together, the whole has an almost musical form. In the opening statement the "grave philosopher"—

Byrd's persona in the commonplace at this stage and one evoked again by the hemlock in the last anecdote—states the main theme. Sexual commerce with women is "the only way for Man to live forever in this world, and that way let us resolve to take." So it is not only sexual desire but also the reproduction of men through progeny, and presumably through male progeny, that obliges men to have to do with women. Male power is, in this sense, compromised from the very start and far into the future. But, as the next anecdote completes the statement of the chief theme, they have us by the balls.

The subsequent entries amplify in mingled form the two major ways in which this is so. By anatomy and otherwise, women are sexually and reproductively more powerful than men. They hardly need men. Or, alternately, sexually they can handle many men but reproductively scarcely need even one. In the realm of anatomy, where the first half of Byrd's entries concentrates its attention, he is stretching to its limits what Thomas Laqueur has called the "one-sex" model of sexual anatomy prevalent in the early eighteenth century. In this model, men's and women's sexual and reproductive parts were seen as analogous, and women's parts were if anything an inferior and inverted version of men's. Male and female orgasms were essentially equivalent and equally necessary to procreation.[16]

Byrd, in a powerful reverse thrust, juxtaposes a substantial clitoris to a penis which in some cases can be "at the most not larger than a moderate clitoris." Further, carried to excess, as it is wont to be, female orgasm is likely to overheat the womb and make it impossible to conceive. Moreover, women can reproduce without or nearly without penetration and by implication reproductively hardly need men at all. Their menstrual blood, which becomes milk, also equips them uniquely to nurture—uniquely, save for some weak men who make an inferior imitation of the female flood of milk. In sum, women become anatomically, biologically, sexually, and reproductively stronger than men, so strong in lust that they risk cancelling their own reproductive powers, while men, with their clitoral penises and feeble trickles of milk in their breasts, can appear as weaker versions of women.

Laqueur implies that this kind of reversal of the flow of anatomical, sexual, and reproductive power is always a possibility within the one-sex model. In such inversions women can become the anatomical standard, somewhat different from men but essentially the superior version of the common form.[17] What Byrd is doing on the level of popular culture or on the level of the users of "scientific" knowledge seems to me however to go a bit beyond this. He is creating an assemblage that prepares the way, in its motivating fears of women and its construction of a female anatomy in some ways distinct from and in all ways superior to the male, for the effort of nineteenth-century physicians to render an explicitly differentiated and unique female sexual anatomy distinctly pathological and *inferior* to male anatomy. For already in the eighteenth century, if Byrd is any indication, anatomy as construed by the consumers of culture was potentially far more deeply and hostilely gendered than the blithe surface of the one-sex model indicates. Male fear of inadequacy, fear of and violence toward women, run as an accompaniment to this terror-driven regendering of anatomy. It took only a slight twist for "scientific medicine," early in the nineteenth century, to turn similar fears and hostilities into a model of a pathologically *weaker* rather than stronger female sexual anatomy.[18]

But, as noted, halfway along Byrd decides that women cannot be both sexually and reproductively stronger than men: lascivious women cannot reproduce. This decision may lead to a certain consistency about women's threat to men that was lacking previously. It becomes clear that lascivious women are the crucial threat to men in both the areas, sexual and reproductive, because they both threaten sexually to consume men and in the process to thwart male reproduction and so block men's chance at immortality. Since most women are lascivious, women are death for men any way you look at it. Such seems to be the implicit logic of the concluding half of Byrd's fulminations.

From this point on, then, superior female reproductive powers disappear from their threatening capacities. So indeed does anatomy altogether. Even virginity, which was earlier seen as at once a potential rejection of men and as something to be guarded lest female desire betray insecure men, and which is in a sense, with menstrual blood, another anatomical uniqueness of women, is no longer on the agenda. The writer's private discourse with his culture reduces to the single item of sexual desire, and desire is rendered as power. In the wars of desire, men must ultimately lose, on a field which, with such champions as Cleopatra and Messalina in the lists, is covered with used-up male lovers. In the case of Semiramis, the field is more tidy because the lovers are buried alive by a ravenous female clever enough to hide the appalling evidences of her insatiability. Annihilation is the end result of man's feebler desire and of his wish to become immortal and so perpetuate his ordering of the world. For males, the consequence is not only death but chaos. Their only hope is to poison themselves so they can resist female desire and, presumably, hope nonetheless for reproduction.

What has really happened here is that the discourse of political power, which runs rampant through this entire commonplace, and which in the writer's entries was always entangled with woman's capriciousness, has now come to be a discourse in which political power and sexual power are one and the same, and a discourse on pure power, the power of order versus disorder.

CHAPTER 2

"THE FEMALE CREED": MISOGYNY ENLIGHTENED?

AT the very moment when he was recording his private fears about himself and about women in his commonplace book, William Byrd was aiming a public dart of misogyny at women in the form of an essay called "The Female Creed," dated to the year 1725. Here, many of the same constructions of women would be offered and if anything deepened into an implied portrait of what Susan Gubar has called "The Female Monster" of the Augustan age. Yet "The Female Creed" is also a curiously gentle satire, and it may foretell an age in which overt, scarifying misogyny was to pass out of fashion. Not out of men's minds, perhaps, or out of their private musings, but out of public discourse.[1] If this is true, then private misogyny of the sort found in Byrd's commonplace was to become one of the last refuges of expression for the intense hatred of women which had hitherto been equally welcome in the public prints.[2]

"The Female Creed" is a parody of the Christian *credo*. In it, the articles of Christian faith are replaced by a list of popular superstitions supposedly held by all women as a virtual religion. These superstitions read like a table of contents to Keith Thomas's well-known study *Religion and the Decline of Magic*, which chronicles the gradual disappearance of such beliefs in the eighteenth, nineteenth, and twentieth centuries.[3] "I believe," says Byrd, speaking for women in what he describes as twenty successive articles of the female faith, "in Spirits, Demons, and Hobgoblins, . . . in Fairy, Pucks, and Robin-good-fellows, . . . in Witches, magicians and sorcerers, . . . in astrologers, coffee-casters and Fortune-tellers, . . . that every man carries his Fate on his Forehead [or in his physiognomy in general], . . . in Dogs, Ravens, and Screech Owls . . . as the most knowing in Futurity, . . . in Dreams, Visions and Impulses by which Guardian Angels and friendly Demons impart timely notices to us of things to come, . . . in Death-watches in a wall & Winding-sheets . . . that are as certain Fore-runners of fate, . . . in . . . the gift of Second-Sight, . . . in the Itching of Sundry Parts about us [which] will make notable discoveries of adventures to come, . . . in Times and Seasons [that] . . . are strangely lucky and others unaccountably unfortunate, . . . that our good or bad Fortune may be clearly collected from the Situation of a Pin upon the Floor, . . . that all odd numbers are lucky except the fatal number of 13 [several headings give examples], . . . and that whoever . . . throws down the Salt at Table will pay for it by some dire misfortune." "In short," concludes this fantastical *credo*, "I believe in the Philosophers-stone, the perpetual motion, the squareing of the circle, the tameing of a Shrew, and what is more incredible than all the rest, I believe in the constancy and Fidelity of Man."

The gentleness of this satire is obvious, as it chides women for what are by this time largely harmless superstitions presumably once held by many and still held by some men, and it ends by suggesting that the most fantastic of women's many unbased beliefs is their trust in men. In due time I will explore the meaning of the public restraint which Byrd is exercising here even as in his private commonplace he is raging against women in general and Charmante in particular. For now, however, we need to note that beneath this polite surface satire "The Female Creed" is easily as full of implicit fury against women as the commonplace book. For each of the twenty presumed articles of female faith listed becomes itself a miniature essay, in which that superstition is loosely linked to a series of gossipy tales about prominent women and men, identified by pseudonyms. Within each essay not only credulous women but also the female body, female desire and power become the introduction to, metaphor for, and implicitly the source of the social and political corruptions of early eighteenth-century England.

As each of these mini-essays proceeds, it is as if a misogynistic and disillusioned William Byrd has seized the speaker's mace from credulous woman, the purported speaker. Under guise of her purported credulity and under the guise of witty court gossip, he is delivering his own increasingly bitter indictment of women and of his times. In the end the link with the particular female superstition with which the mini-essay had begun is nearly lost, dissolving into far-reaching ridicule of women and of English society and politics.

I believe in astrologers, coffee-casters, and Fortune-tellers of every denomination, whether they profess to read the Ladys destiny in their faces, in their palms, or like those of China in their fair posteriors. I believe according as the Planets and Fixt stars happen to be placed in the sky at the Instant of our birth, they forebode what complexion we shall be of, and what is to betide us every year of our lives. I believe my Lady Pilfer cou'd by no means help being light-finger'd, and lifting Fans and china-cups, every time she went to Mother Tomb's, because that Knave Mercury was lord of her ascendant, nor can Furistante well avoid being a vixen and a Termagant, yea and exceeding loud in her Curtain lectures, because she happen'd to be born under Mars, which all the sons of art know to be a boistrous Planet, and since that wanton Huzzy Venus presided at the nativity of poor Miss Frail, how cruel are the Prudes, for allowing no Quarter to that unfortunate Damsel, because she happen'd to prove more fruitfull than themselves. I believe tho' the Stars hold their heads so high they some times condescend to act the low part of Jonathan Wild, and help People to their gold snuff boxes and Silver Spoons again, that like the Maiden Sisters in St. James' street they kindly bring the Sexes together, and get many a hearty curse for their pains. I firmly believe that casting of Coffee Grounds is a very thriving branch of the Black Art and by the grotesque Figures drawn by Some invisible Painter in the cup, shews the Fortune of the caster pretty plain, but not quite so evidently as the believeing it shews his Folly. I believe from my heart that the Pretender to the crowne of Great Britain has no other hopes of ever putting it on his head, but what the Mistresses of this art inspire him with. I believe if a Bull or a Goat appear in a mans cup, he must needs be a Whoremaster, tho' he be a Lord Chancellor or an Arch-Bishop, and if a Bear or a Munky be seen in a Ladys she'll need a vast deal of Grace to keep her honest. If an ass or an owl chance to be there, the happy caster will have a fair Hit to be an alderman, but if the Beast's ears appear longer, or the Bird's countenance graver than ordinary, there are hopes he may come to be a Judge or at lowest a Sergeant at Law. If a ravening wolfe be in the cup, the man may rise in the navy and grow to be a Captain of a man of War, or if he be a Land officer, and good for nothing else, he may live to be a Governour in His Majesty's Plantations. A Dutch mastiff or a Parrot are ill omens in a woman's cup and foretell she'll continue long a pure Virgin and grow as censorious and discreet as Mademoiselle Sky who is so vigorous a Prude she wont suffer a male creature in her house that has not been serv'd like Seresini.

The satire placed under this heading is not as hard on women as that found under others, but "Lady Pilfer," "Furistante," and "Miss Frail" leave no doubt that superstition is far from the only female sin. From degraded women, the narrative proceeds to Lord Chancellors, Archbishops, aldermen and Judges, any of whom may be revealed by the coffee grounds to be a whoremaster or an ass. Having potentially indicted the entire English political and religious establishment, Byrd moves on to a personal grievance, letting the shape of a "ravening wolf" in the bottom of the coffee cup stand for military men, one of whom "if he be a Land officer, and good for nothing else, he may live to be a Governour in His Majesty's Plantations." This is a clear reference to Alexander Spotswood, an officer who had served in the English army in France and been rewarded with the lieutenant governorship of Virginia in 1709 at a time Byrd had coveted that post. Byrd's subsequent efforts to unseat Spotswood had by 1719 led to an ignominious rejection of his claims by English authorities, a failure he is still trying to overcome in his commonplace book in the

1720's. The sources of this colonial's alienation from the establishment are here laid bare. The miniature narrative then concludes with "Mademoiselle Sky," who, in the opposite sin from "Miss Frail," tolerates only men who, like the Italian male soprano Seresini, have been castrated. Superstition, then, is merely the gate through which female failings become the setting, and, in the case of "Lady Pilfer" and "Miss Frail" the model and metaphor, for Byrd's indictment of the ravening wolves and whoremasters in power in England.

But the satire of women becomes far harsher in later references, and it soon becomes the fallible, repulsive, and implicitly corruptible female body itself that is the central metaphor for all these tales of social and political corruption. Section after section of "The Female Creed" goes out of its way to dwell on the weaknesses of women's bodies, as each section moves on toward its larger function of satirizing English power in general. Women's inability to control their bodily functions fascinates the writer. In the context of the ongoing social and political satire Byrd is pushing here, these references seem to stand for an England that has lost its morals and continence.

Hence it comes to pass that so many Females in all countrys can scarce hold their precious water, haveing been terrify'd in the Nursery with Bulbeggars and Apparitions. This is the case of the unfortunate Dripabunda, who when She fancy'd She saw the Ghost of her deceast Husband, dy'd away for fear the good man was come to life again. From that fatal moment she lost her Retentive faculty, beyond the Relief of Turpentine Pills and Bristolwater, nor can even Dr. Friend, or Apollo himself intirely stop the Leak, but stil whenever she laughs beyond a Simper or a Broad Smile, the liveing Salalmoniac flows from her.

But then alas if the fatal Point of the Pin lye towards a poor Girle, every thing that day will fall out wrong, she cannot stoop but she'l squeeze out a f--t, or laugh but she'll be-piss her self.

But Enthusiasts tell us we are most dispos'd to see visions when we [women] are fasting and full of Wind, our souls being then most alert and aptest to ramble out of our Bodys.

Recommend me to discreet Fartamira, who never pretends to wipe her Backside on Such a day as this, for fear of bedaubing her taper Fingers. I was acquainted with a wise Woman once, who always kept her bed on Childermass day, believing her Self safe in that Snugg Situation, but that precaution fail'd her once very cruelly. For poor Mrs. Straddle, (the Gentlewoman's name) pearching with all her weight upon the Pot, the brittle Utensil flew to pieces, filling the Bed with water of high-perfume. . . .

Typically, these references lead on to larger satirical purposes; in the latter case, for example, fashionable London in general, and in specific the speculators who profited from the South Sea Bubble, are the ultimate images of loss of control.[4]

At moments "The Female Creed" could be called "The Female Posterior," so great is Byrd's fascination with this aspect of repulsive female corporeality.

I believe these Elfs to shew their love of Cleanliness, wou'd pinch a dirty Slut every night, til her Haunches were as black as a Gammon of Bacon, so that if Drabella or Fustimina had liv'd in those cleanly days, their nether Parts had been nippt to a Jelly.

But alas if a Female chance to be markt on either Breast like Miss Tinder or upon either Buttock, like the widdow Touchwood, tis odds but she'll be troubled with a Devil, which nothing but Fasting and Prayer will be able to cast out.

Tis a certain piece of History that Mademoiselle Frizzle was 26 years ago put into so mortal a Fright with one of these Deathwatches, that her very heart-breakers, that lay upon her Toilet, turn'd as grey as a Gander, yet blessed be God she is stil alive, and strong enough to open her Self a passage to the King with her Elbows, every Drawing-room night let the Throng be never so great, and she may stil receive her pension, and carry that hideous Smile upon her face full 30 years longer, because the fatal Insect tickt 56 times.

. . . at such a Sullen time as this, tis impossible even for Miss Tidy, who dos every thing with a grace, to dress her head to her mind, either the plaits will lye eneaven or the Poke Stand quite ascue, and let her Maid be never so carefull, when she pins up her Gown, she'll unavoidably run a calker into her thrummy Breech.

Yet uncontrolled bodily functions and repulsive gluteal corporeality only stand for the fact that it is the female body in general which is portrayed as repulsive, dirty, and ugly in a theme which is prior to, permeates, and prefigures the larger, nongendered social critique Byrd is offering.

In the first place I believe that Dreams like the excessive modesty of Prudes or the overacted Grief of Widdows are to be taken by the contrarys. . . .

So Seignior Tetato dreamt last summer at Tunbridge, that the great Dutch Woman patted him on the Cheak with her Shoulder of Mutton hand, and the next morning the Queen of the Fairys frown'd upon him.

Her Ladyship ran nimbly up stairs, to gain the more time for Conversation, and surpriz'd the unfortunate Madam Pitapat dirty and undrest, with no more light in the Room than what the Fire and her Eyes afforded.

Fine Mrs Lurewell Understands the power of this lucky number, and knows she shall give most pain when she wears but one Patch. For this reason she never Sticks on more on a Sunday morning when she gos to church, tho' she have never so many Pimples to conceal.

Immediately upon this Disaster, a grave Aldermans Lady, who was indeed old and ugly enough to be a Witch, bad him beware, or Some mischief wou'd betide him. Voracio instead of being thankfull for this sage admonition, only answer'd her Lad[p] with a very ingenious Horselaugh not having time to wast upon idle Repartees. But the omen Soon overtook him.

It goes without saying that the lust of these repulsive creatures for food, sex, and power is also a distinguishing characteristic of the women portrayed in these gossipy passages.

My good Lady Junket . . . once refus'd to tast a Pye, because it had 13 ortolans in it, and this too when Lent was just ended, and there was not a morsel of any think else for Supper. How unfortunate was the Curiosity which made her Lad[p] inquire how many of those rare Birds were immur'd in the Crust? But certain it is, that the moment her question was answer'd, She lay'd down her Knife & Fork, retir'd from the Table, and pretended she cou'd not eat, tho' her poor Guts croakt all the while at their disappointment.

It was in one of these morning-slumbers that the agreable Decora fancey'd she saw count Gimcrack rideing Bare-backt upon a colt which galloping up directly to her, cast his feeble Rider plumb into her lap.

I believe when a young Gentlewoman's Elbow itches, she will shortly steal out of bed from her Sister, like Miss Fondlefellow, & notwithstanding her pretended fear of Spirits, go in quest of a more Significant Bedfellow.

So very frail is the strongest female Resolution, at a time when all the humours of the Body flow to the weakest part, and all the passions of the Soul are ripen'd into Love. I believe that the prime Season for Critical minutes, is the merry month of May, because then the Sap rises in the animal as briskly as in the vegetable World.

So Scarrouel while she was a penniless Poets Wife, and consequently kept pretty sharp, had a strong Impulse she shou'd live to carry the Grand Monarch about in Leading-strings and Since the decease of that prodigious Woman, tis said her neice Violetta has had another, that she shall do the same thing by a monarch grander than he.

Clearly the misogynistic agenda of "The Female Creed" runs well beyond the superstition that its title and organizing rubrics assign to women. Women are the very essence of human corruption. Only once this portrait is firmly established within each heading's essay does Byrd go on to attack corruption in the male establishment.

Squire Sparerib has reason to think 7 a happy number, because he repents duly once in Seaven years, of haveing made so many Cuckolds in the city, and so many Cullys at the other end of the Towne. The reason of his Septennial Repentance is plain, he suspects every 7th year to be something of a Climacterick, and consequently to threaten his life. When this sad Revolution comes on, the poor 'Squire is in great agonys, he fasts his Scragged Carcass to a Skeleton, and out-prays a repenting Harlot. If then he stink for fear at the approach of the Smaller Climactericks, he'll surely dye for fear, when the great one stares him in the face.

A mole under the ingenious Jack Shepherd's left Ear portended he'd come at last, where most Ministers of state deserve to come, to the Gallows.

Thus the day had hardly dawned, when Majr. Bluster dreamt that the Devil, dwellt perpetually on his lips, took him up by the chin, with a Promise to shew him London, but disappointed him sore, and shew'd him Tiburn.

So that great Oracle of Equity, Count Bribantio had a vast partiality for Five, provided it had three significant cyphers after it. Insomuch that whenever his Eys happen'd to be dazzled with this charming number, especially when it cou'd be made Guineas, his Whigg-Integrity all forsook him in an instant. Under so powerfull a temptation he cou'd not forbear prostituting the Kings conscience of which he was the unworthy Keeper, and quite forgot that he was the Guardian of the Widdow and the Fatherless.

What William Byrd is really constructing in "The Female Creed" is a precocious version of the metaphor of "The Female Monster" that Swift, Pope, and others of their circle were to use to great effect in the years immediately succeeding Byrd's essay. In their hands as well, female corporeality, corruptibility, and desire became a metaphor for social corruption in general, and so a vehicle for a social criticism that ranged far beyond women. As Susan Gubar puts it, some of the scriblerians' women are "corroding matter personified." Further, "the debased arts of the female serve . . . as an emblem of the corruption of literary and ethical standards in Walpole's England."[5] In effect, Swift and Pope are to combine the entropic, annihilating qualities of women as seen in Byrd's commonplace with the bodily corruption and continuing, possessive desire he pictures in "The Female Creed" into a single female monster whose vices—formlessness, mundanity, corruption, insatiability—stand for those of Augustan England. It appears from these cases that in early eighteenth-century England misogyny, self-fear, and social and political alienation were being combined in the minds of marginal men, first of William Byrd, a rejected colonial, and then of Swift and Pope, the Tory artists isolated amidst the corruptions of Walpole's England, into a portrait of pervasive horror whose name, or at least whose central metaphor, was woman.

The William Byrd of the commonplace is thus readily recognizable in the William Byrd of "The Female Creed." Yet above its scabrous interior "The Female Creed" remains the somewhat gentler satire of women implied in its title and list of outdated superstitions. On this level it makes the superficial but I think meaningful assertion that women are simply repositories of superstition. This accusation in some ways goes back as far as the *Malleus Maleficarum*, but is not in and of itself a devastating criticism.[6] What is going on here? Why is the intense misogyny of "The Female Creed" cloaked in such a polite guise?

What is going on, I would suggest, is that William Byrd is in the process of entering the enlightenment. We know this from several immediately succeeding sources. The final pages of his commonplace book, written around 1726, are dominated by a compendium of factual knowledge, a proposal for a universal language, and an entranced commentary on William Wollaston's *The Religion of Nature Delineated*, itself an effort to construct a rational science of ethics. As a result, on balance the commonplace is no longer an Erasmian commonplace, almost exclusively filled with rhetorical/moral poses and witty court gossip from across the centuries. Instead, it becomes the mnemonic and reflective instrument of a man occupied with useful facts, with schemes for improvement and with the power of reason. These are the very characteristics of practical enlightenment thought. Shortly thereafter, on returning to Virginia in 1726, Byrd confirmed his entry into at least the language and possibly the very cosmology of the enlightenment by describing himself in effect as first mover of his plantation world:

> Like one of the patriarchs, I have my flocks and my herds, my bondmen, and bondwomen, and every soart of trade amongst my own servants, so that I live in a kind of independance on every one, but Providence. However tho' this soart of life is without expence yet it is attended with a great deal of trouble. I must take care to keep all my people to their duty, to set all the springs in motion, and to make every

one draw his equal share to carry the machine forward. But then tis an amusement in this silent country, and a continual exercise of our patience and oeconomy.

A few years later he was to abandon his earlier defense of slavery and denounce the practice in terms congenial to a new mentality of secular enlightened benevolence, as a violation of the humanity of slaves and masters alike. He even spelled out the solution for this evil practice, an end to the trade in human beings.[7] The old Tory William Byrd begins to sound more like Thomas Jefferson, the genius of the American enlightenment.

But we note that to be "enlightened," to speak in terms of abstract first-mover deities and of a secular, rational ethics, was in Byrd's mind in no way inconsistent with the continuation of his own patriarchal power. In fact, the passage in which he depicts himself as first mover invokes that metaphor and the new, mechanistic cosmology which it implies in the service of a stronger image of patriarchy. As first mover the plantation patriarch is no mere biblical figure—though this archaic metaphor is also employed. Rather, he is lifted above the level of mere master, even of biblical father, to the status of a distant deity, whose mere motion is enough to set all the microcosms of the plantation in constant and effective motion for an implied eternity. An effective metaphor indeed! Byrd as first mover is a lofty, distant, immensely powerful creator of a patriarch. In this patriarch's mind the enlightenment could be appropriated not only to ornament his intellect but also to amplify his authority. In the end, it was authority which mattered most to him, as Byrd the enlightened patriarch never freed his slaves but kept them on his plantation as tiny cogwheels in the miniature cosmos which his authority had set in motion.

"The Female Creed" stands at the beginning of William Byrd's impending entry into and appropriation of the enlightenment. In it, he is conducting the initial act of appropriation, the seizure of the newly desacralized cosmology, of the new faith in science, reason, and improvement, by men, or by this man at least, as an asset eventually to be used for his own patriarchal purposes. What we see is of course not the seizure itself, but a reciprocal act by which an about-to-become-enlightened man lifts up in his hands all the "superstitions" of the past age, and consigns them to women. Essentially he is feminizing superstition in order to take masculine possession of the rationality of the enlightenment.[8]

Where did he get the idea? Byrd's own library, though he probably did not have it all with him in London at the time, contained works that treated popular beliefs, witchcraft, fairies, etc., in considerable detail.[9] Such incompletely identified works as *Unheard of Curiosities*, *Miscellanea Curiosa*, *History of the Magicians*, and *Apparitions*, all found in the later catalog of his library, very likely treated many beliefs that were even then becoming "superstitions." Also in his library were *Frauds of the Monks* and Loyd's *Popery*, which linked magical and superstitious beliefs to Catholicism, a common association which Byrd also makes. Ben Jonson's works were known to Byrd as well and Jonson's poems include details of fairy behavior found also in "The Female Creed." Sir William Temple's *oeuvre* was in Byrd's library as well, and Temple wrote on popular beliefs, including fairies, Puck, and Robin-good-fellow. Joseph Glanville's study of *Witchcraft* covered nicely, and skeptically, details of demonology also found in Byrd's essay.[10] Other popular beliefs, especially of the upper classes, such as coffee-casting, the Philosopher's stone, and perpetual motion, were surely known to Byrd from experience.

There is a strong suspicion that the catalyst that led Byrd to write "The Female Creed" was Henry Bourne's *Antiquitates Vulgares*. This book appears not to have been in Byrd's library—unless it is mistitled as *Antiquitates Christianae*; his books frequently had partially incorrect spine titles and in this case the misnomer would be appropriate to Bourne's intention (see below)—but it first appeared in 1725, just when "The Female Creed" was written. Its encyclopedic form matches that taken by Byrd's essay, and nearly *all* the arcane details of the very first article of the "Creed," beginning "I believe, as all good Catholicks ought to do, in Spirits, Demons, and Hobgoblins," are found in chapters 6, 8, 10, and 11 of Bourne and are seldom found so closely woven together in other sources.[11] If Bourne was Byrd's inspiration, the transmutation the Virginian worked on his source is interesting. Bourne was an Anglican curate who attributed the vulgar beliefs he chronicled to ordinary men and women alike. His object was characteristic of the early enlightenment, namely to cleanse popular life of ceremonies based on beliefs "almost all superstitious, being generally either the produce of Heathenism; or the Inventions of Indolent Monks, who having nothing else to do, were the Forgers of many silly and wicked Opinions, to keep the World in Awe and Ignorance."[12] Some popular beliefs, however, he considered either socially functional or consistent with a latitudinarian Anglicanism. Here, he felt that his aim "to wipe off . . . the Dust they have contracted, to clear them of Superstition, and make known their End and Design, may turn [them] to some Account, and be of Advantage."[13] Byrd in turn culled out from Bourne and from other readings only beliefs worthy of scorn, and attributed them to women. He was that eager to consign the magical past to women, because only by so doing could he stand secure in a masculinized, enlightened rationality.

There was a terrible irony in this action, for what William Byrd thereby assigned to women was not only the world of magic and wonder in which European men and women had lived since before history began, but also his own personal past. He was fleeing as fast as he could from the frightened, credulous William Byrd who, on June 21, 1710, had recorded: "About five nights since I dreamed I saw a flaming star in the air at which I was much frightened and called some others to see it but when they came it disappeared. I fear this portends some judgement to this country or at least to myself." There had been several such apocalyptic dreams and portents in Byrd's early life, as he adjusted to the high mortality of Virginia after his first return there in 1705 as a young man of thirty. At one point he was to dig up his dead father and try to read a message of death and redemption in the corpse's face.[14] As late as 1716 in London he would go to a "conjurer," a fortune-teller, at a time when he was having still more prophetic dreams.[15] Now, less than ten years later, a maritally and politically defeated and probably no more confident William Byrd was seizing new truths, the truths of reason and improvement, to save himself from oblivion. To consolidate his progress in this endeavor he dumped on women as mere "superstition" the articles of his own former faith, namely prophetic dreams, visions, signs, conjurers, fortune-tellers, the lot: "I [Woman] believe in astrologers, coffee-casters and Fortune-tellers of every denomination. . . . I believe in Dreams, Visions, and Impulses by which Guardian Angels and Friendly Demons impart timely notices to us of things to come." Through this opened door, a door into his own past, really, he poured scorn on "superstitious" women for their bodies as well. In exorcising women he was exorcising his own past beliefs and revealing his fears about himself, the fear that he was not modern enough, the fear, perhaps, that his own body and self were corruptible. Such was the psychology of "rational" empowerment for this man.

Just for the record, what was the exact nature of the new world that William Byrd was masculinizing and scrambling to enter, the reciprocal of his indictment of "female" superstition as embodied in "The Female Creed"? A world without mystery; a world without supernatural beings save a distant, first-moving deity, with no fairies, no witches, no Puck, no Robin-good-fellow; a world with no fate in its stars, unable to foretell its future, in which coffee grounds were but scrap and animals not portents but only organisms; a world in which the body held no signs but only scientifically understandable mechanisms; a world without prophetic dreams and visions; in which death watch beetles were just a species that ate wood, candle smoke mere pollution without images of the future in it, and an itch just a tremor of the nerves, a sign of nothing more; a world in which time was uniform and without auspicious or fateful moments, a pin just a pin, a number just a quantity, and spilled salt something to be swept up; a world with no Philosopher's stone, and in which the circle was forever unsquareable in the light of modern mathematics. But perhaps he did not see it in this cold light: to William Byrd the enlightenment was mostly fashion and power.

I have called the misogyny implied in this discarding of former selves and former intellectual fashions, and in the dumping of these on women, "gentle." You may wonder why, since it reveals the gendered savagery of a man scrambling to be intellectually fashionable, and hides in its subtexts a hatred of the female body even deeper than that being entered concurrently in his commonplace book. Yet in the end it is gentle, for in the end Byrd's ultimate accusation against women is that they are intellectually unfashionable. While this charge hoists lustful and possessive woman on her own petard by consigning her to be that which she most fears, unfashionable, it is, in and of itself, not a vicious attack on women. Compared to what lay beneath the surface, buried in Byrd's commonplace or deep in the body of the "Creed" itself, an outdated superstition is a gentle rubric for identifying women. And my question is, why? Why, in an age soon to be noted for the savagery of its public as well as private misogyny, did William Byrd in public discourse feel it best to subsume his deeper purposes under the relatively gentle misogynistic accusation that women were at best unfashionable and at worst irrational?

There were surely several reasons but, for what it is worth, I think one of them is that he had no choice. The reason for this is connected with the nature of the enlightenment itself. I would suggest, very tentatively, that a worldview known for its benevolence, optimism, and faith in human reason, could not, at least on the surface, long continue to indulge openly and primarily in the vicious sexual, corporeal misogyny that made women a race of inhuman, lustful, annihilating demons. Demons were, as "The Female Creed" demonstrates, passing out of fashion, so female demons likewise were no longer acceptable. Moreover, a creed, the enlightenment, known for its optimism could hardly continue to indulge in public in explicit nightmare visions of female entropy. Finally, the new faith in human rationality would eventually imply for some enlightenment thinkers at least the potential rationality of both genders and all races. Women could not automatically be considered an utterly irrational, totally separate race. So I would suggest that Swift and Pope, these Tory misogynists, were the last of a dying breed, the public and coruscating misogynist, the crafter of feral female demons, of gendered nightmares and entropic disorders. And I would suggest that the gentler satire that provides the largest frame for "The Female Creed," and beneath whose mild headings Byrd hides his severer misogynies, reflects William Byrd's subliminal awareness that just as superstition was going out of style in a new age, so was raw, public misogyny. If he wanted to appropriate the enlightenment, he had to be at least superficially polite to women. Hatred was delegated to his subtext.

The enlightenment cut both ways, of course. Byrd's subtexted hatred of female corporeality was partly related to the personal frustrations over access to power and resources taken up in his commonplace book, but it was also itself enhanced by his very movement into the early enlightenment. What he was exorcising, in "woman's" voice, which was really his own voice, was "woman" in himself in all its dimensions, the superstitious and the corporeal, the credulous and the corruptible, the frivolous and the fleshly self. All this was preparation for his entry into the disembodied, benevolent rationality of a new cosmology, a cosmology which he had masculinized by rejecting with contempt all that was superstitious or corporeal, even within himself, as "female." But all these operations were nonetheless subsumed under the general tone of civility with which an enlightened man had to treat women in public discourse.

Private misogyny was, however, another matter. In 1725, in his commonplace book, William Byrd still felt free to cast the war of the sexes not only as anatomical and sexual but as a virtual race war of annihilation whose stakes were order and disorder. Forty years later, so did one of his successors in Virginia.

CHAPTER 3

COMMONPLACES II: THOMAS JEFFERSON

WILLIAM BYRD was not alone in the intensely misogynistic vision rendered in his commonplace. That view of women evidently persisted in private male discourse for some time, as at least one further case testifies. Thomas Jefferson's literary commonplace book from the 1750's, 60's, and 70's has just been properly edited and its entries dated.[1] One episode in it is startlingly similar.

Jefferson's is, like Byrd's, a genteel commonplace book. Its entries are designed to embody those rhetorics and understandings of the social and moral world a gentleman would need. These entries are, however, a far cry from the usual brief, unsourced and paraphrased rhetorical/moral attitudes practiced in William Byrd's encounter with his culture. To Byrd as to Erasmus, knowledge lay chiefly in an almost randomly arranged series of moral postures as these were embodied in anecdotes about famous persons from the past. Such tales were found in miscellaneous compilations. Moral knowledge lay in rendering partially into the transcriber's own rhetoric this panoply of past behavior and remarks. Jefferson's book has another and essentially Lockean epistemology. That is, while Jefferson does not literally follow Locke's advice to enter accurate quotations under subject headings, naming the sources and indexing the headings, he does name his sources and quotes them accurately and sometimes at length.[2] Moreover, the sources are seldom anecdotes about the famous, but rather are passages from ancient and modern literature, drama, and political philosophy. In the end he organized them not by subject exactly but certainly by genre. This is what the modern age would regard as a more serious book. The accurately quoted and sourced, frequently extended passages from serious modern genres imply an enlightenment epistemology. They imply a critical mentality attuned to the exact formulations employed by recognized but generally fairly recent authorities and implicitly invite critical appraisal as well. Knowledge becomes a scientific discourse, a thing to be rendered, compared, and criticized with precision.

Yet curiously this new epistemology is undercut by the fact that many of Jefferson's sources lie in "literature," in the English poets and playwrights of the seventeenth and eighteenth centuries. In Jefferson the ancient idea that great utterances can be ennobling—and he includes many such—slides easily into the modern idea that fine literature contains many passages of wisdom and inspiration to be admired. Neither of these conceptions does much to enhance the critical mentality otherwise implied in his Lockean practice of long, accurate, and specifically sourced quotations. A long, accurate quotation from Milton, for example, is there to establish attitudes and to be admired more than to be compared and challenged, and in this respect differs little from the moral rhetoric of the ancients. Knowledge from literature is nearly as static as knowledge from classical apothegms. Particularly in its earliest citations, Jefferson's commonplace is more deeply akin to Byrd's than its Lockean precisions indicate.[3]

It is more deeply akin still, in that its first citations, entered between 1756 and 1764, are dominated by outbursts of quotations in which rage against arbitrary power alternates with a startling misogyny. Remember, too, as I assemble some of these for you, that Jefferson later (1768) and in a more mellow mood edited his own commonplace, and these are the early entries he left *in*.[4]

What seems to be the earliest of these intense bursts of quotations on rebellion and misogyny has been dated from Jefferson's handwriting and original pagination to the years 1756–1762, when he was between thirteen and nineteen years old. This outburst accounts for roughly forty of the eighty-odd earliest quotations from these years, entries which Jefferson kept when he edited the commonplace in 1768. In essence it occurs as two brief runs of quotations alternating with sequences that are not misogynistic or rebellious, but rather treat a wide variety of more conventional topics. In the two runs of quotations we are concerned with, passages evoking a struggle against overweening power, rebellion, disharmony, and death are intermingled with quotations that, taken together, are at best deeply ambivalent about women.

Here, as always, Jefferson draws one or several quotations from each of his sources, then moves on to the next. Within each work Jefferson draws from—Milton's *Paradise Lost*, for example—the quotations as I give them are almost certainly still in the order he originally copied them in. While there is no guarantee, the order of quotations *across* the various authors and works used, as presented here, appears to be the same order in which these works were originally excerpted. What appears to have happened later, in 1768, is that Jefferson dropped all the quotations from certain works, while moving the quotations from a few others, read later, back among these early entries from 1756–1762. Those which were dropped represent excisions which can never be recovered. I have omitted the later entries which in 1768 Jefferson moved back among his earlier entries, but which were not part of his original sequence. Thus, the specific quotations given here are probably both in their original order and in the order Jefferson himself gave them in 1768.

Jefferson draws first and most deeply on Milton, an author whose ambivalence toward women is well known, but here the Virginian is using the more modulated *Paradise Lost* rather than *Samson Agonistes*, that fable of symbolic emasculation. He begins with a classic series in which the protagonist is the rebel angel, Satan.

——What tho the Field be lost?
All is not lost; the unconquerable Will,
And Study of Revenge, immortal Hate
And Courage never to submit or yield:
And what is else not to be overcome?
. . . To bow & Sue for Grace
With suppliant Knee, & deifie his Po[wer,]
Who from the Terrour of this Arm: so late
Doubted his Empire, that were low ind[eed,]
That were an Ignominy, & Shame benea[th]
This Downfall.——

Id: I. 105. [No. 219 in the Wilson Edition]

——But of this be sure
To do ought Good never will be our Tas[k,]
But ever to do Ill our sole Delight,
As being contrary to his high Will
Whom we resist.——

I[d: I. 158.] [No. 220, Wilson]

Here we may reign secure, & in my Choice
To reign is worth Ambition tho' in Hell,
Better to reign in Hell, than serve in Heaven.

Lib: I. I:261. [No. 221]

——But he his wonted pride
Soon recollecting, with high words that bore
Semblance of Worth, not Substance, gently rais'd
Their fainting Courage, & dispell'd their Fears.

Id: I. 527. [No. 222]

——Our better Part remains
To work in close Design, by Fraud or Guile,
What Force effected not: that he no less
At length from us may find, who overcomes
By Force, hath overcome but half his Foe.

Lib: I. v. 645. [No. 223]

——though in this vast Recess,
Free, & to none accountable, preferring
Hard Liberty before the easy Yoke
of servile Pomp.

Lib: 2. v. 254. [No. 224]

Clearly, death and destruction await the rebel, who gladly risks these and challenges the highest authority, in order to be free, even if free in hell. The final quotation sets a tone which will be picked up again and again in the quotations recorded in these years: "preferring Hard Liberty before the easy Yoke of servile Pomp." Please note that Jefferson is only fifteen to nineteen years old at this time, and the Stamp Act is not yet an issue, so there is no obvious political reference here. If these passages resonate for specific reasons with Jefferson's life, it is for reasons unrelated to politics as ordinarily understood.

Immediately thereafter appear two quotations (with two others separating them) that invoke an idealized picture of married love, albeit with a final injunction that "love unlibidinous" is the condition of avoiding a lover's hell.

Nor gentle purpose, nor endearing smiles
Wanted, nor youthful dalliance as beseems
Fair couple, linkt in happy nuptial league,
Alone as they.—

Milt. Par. L. 4. 337. [No. 225]

——but in those hearts
Love unlibidinous reign'd, nor jealousy
Was understood, the injur'd lover's hell.

id. 5. 448. [No. 228]

A new series of quotations on struggle, oblivion, heaven, and hell follows, still from *Paradise Lost,* and then comes a whole series from the same source that focuses on women and considerably less favorably than previously. The first of these speaks of the inherent disharmony between unequals, and is not specifically gendered, yet in context it may imply some sort of gender conflict. The context is established by the ensuing four entries, in which women are seen beneath their outward show to be seducers and temptresses, who must be subjected to a strong man lest they subject him, and seen to be creatures who, if unrestrained by men, are evil.

Among Unequals what Society
Can sort, what Harmony or true Delight?
. . . in Disparity
The one intense, the other still remiss
Cannot well suit with either, but soon prove
Tedious alike:——Id: 1: 383. [No. 234]

——here Passion first I felt,
Commotion strange, in all Enjoyments else
Superior & unmov'd, here only weak
Against the Charm of Beautie's powerful Glan[ce.]
Or Nature fail'd in me, & left some Part
Not Proof Enough such Object to sustain,
Or from my Side subducting, took perhaps
More than enough; at least on her bestow'd
Too much of Ornament, in outward Shew
Elaborate:——Id: 1: 530. [No. 235]

For what admir'st thou, what transports thee s[o?]
An Outside? fair no Doubt, & worthy well
Thy cherishing, thy honouring, & thy Love,
Not thy Subjection: . . .
. . . Oft-times nothing profits more
Than Self-esteem, grounded on just & right
Well manag'd; of that Skill the more thou know['st]
The more she will acknowledge thee her Head,
And to Realities yield all her Shows: . . .
Id: 1: 567. [No. 236]

For he who tempts, though in vain, at least asperses
The tempted with Dishonour foul, suppos'd
Not incorruptible of Faith, not Proof
[Against Temptation.—B: 9. 1. 296.] [No. 237]

——Thus it shall befal
Him who to Worth in Women overtrusting
Lets her Will rule; restraint she will not brook,
And left to herself, if Evil thence ensue,
She first his weak Indulgence will accuse.
Id: 1: 1182. [No. 238]

In these initial entries, then, quotations expressing rage alternate with quotations discussing women ever less favorably. These are followed in turn by several of what is to become a long series of entries that definitely seems to have some sort of personal reference. One speaks of a past that cannot be recalled or undone; the second of a father's doom—meaning perhaps both his fate and his decisions—which is set and irreversible, and then of a wistful longing to lay the head "in my Mothers Lap," an act made impossible by the father's dreadful sentence.

But past who can recall, or done undo?
Not God omnipotent, nor Fate.——
Id: 1: 926. [No. 239]

Be it so! for I submit; His Doom is fair,
That Dust I am, & shall to Dust return.
O welcome Hour whenever! Why delays
His Hand to execute, what His Decree
Fix'd on this Day? Why do I over-live?
Why am I mock'd with Death, & lengthen'd out
To deathless Pain? How gladly would I meet
Mortality my Sentence, & be Earth
Insensible! How glad would lay me down,
As in my Mother's Lap! There I should rest
And in sleep secure: His dreadful Voice no more
Would thunder in my Ears:——
B: 10. 1: 769. [No. 240]

This is followed immediately by one of Milton's most famous tirades against women, so powerful that it must speak for itself:

——[I was] imagin'd wise,
Constant, mature, proof against all Assaults:

And understood not all was but a Shew,
Rather than solid Virtue; all but a Rib,
Crooked by Nature, bent (as now appears)
More to the Part sinister from me drawn;
Well if thrown out, as supernumerary
To my just Number found!—O! why did God[,]
Creator wise! that Peopl'd highest Heav'n
With Spirits masculine, create at last
This Novelty on Earth, this fair Defect
Of Nature? And not fill the World at once
With Men, as Angels, without feminine?
Or find some other Way to generate
Mankind? This Mischeif had not then befall['n,]
And more that shall befal: innumerable
Disturbances on Earth through female Snares,
And straight Conjunction with this Sex!——
[Id: 1: 881] [No. 241]

Milton's startling wish that God had not created women, and had given men some other way to generate mankind, so that they could escape the sinister mischief women cause, is going to be echoed in implicit and explicit form by several other authors in these early pages of Jefferson's commonplace. Seductive women are then followed by death, as the excerpts from *Paradise Lost* draw to a rather grim close:

——let us make short,
Let us seek *Death*:—or, he not found, supply
With our own Hands his Office on ourselves.
Why stand we longer shivering unde Fears,
That shew no End but Death; & have the Pow'r
Of many Ways to die, the shortest chusing,
Destruction with Destruction to Destroy?
Id: 1: 1000. [No. 242]

But have I now seen Death? is this the Way
I must return to native Dust? O Sight
Of Terror, foul, & ugly to behold,
Horrid to think, how horrible to feel.
B: II. 1: 462. [No. 243]

A bit later, after many excerpts from other sources and on other subjects, Jefferson begins a second round by turning first to Shakespeare. From the vast and varied folds of the bard's rhetorical cloak he draws forth more quotations on struggle, rebellion, freedom, and death. Women do not explicitly enter the scene just yet, but it does begin to dawn on the reader that the young man selecting these passages is quite obsessed with power and rebellion in his own life, else why out of all English literature give *Paradise Lost* and *Julius Caesar* so much space, and why mine them almost exclusively for quotations in this Cassian vein?

Cowards die many Times before their Deaths;
The valiant never taste of Death but once.
Of all the Wonders that I yet have heard,
It seems to me most strange that Men should fear
Seeing that Death, a necessary End,
Will come when it will come.——
Julius Caesar. Act. 2. Scene 4. [No. 268]

Must I give Way & Room to your rash Choler?
Shall I be frighted when a Madman stares?

—— —— ——

——Fret 'till your proud Heart break:
Go, shew your Slaves how choleric you are,
And make your Bondmen tremble. Must I budge?
Must I observe you? Must I stand & crouch
Under your testy Humour? By the Gods,
You shall digest the Venom of your Spleen,
Tho' it do split you: For from this Day forth,
I'll use you for my Mirth, yea, for my Laughter,
When you are waspish.——
Id: Act 4: S: 3. [No. 269]

Do not presume too much upon my Love;
I may do that I shall be sorry for.
Id: [No. 270]

I cannot tell, what you & other Men
Think of this Life; but for my single self,

I had as lief not be, as live to be
In Awe of such a Thing as I myself.
I was born free as Caesar, so were you;
We both have fed as well; & we can both
Endure the Winter's cold as well as he.

—— —— —— ——

—— ——This Man
Is now become a God; & Cassius is
A wretched Creature, & must bend his Body,
If Caesar carelessly but nod on him.
Id: Act: 1. Sc: 3. [No. 271]

——Hold my Hand:
Be factious for Redress of all these Griefs,
And I will set this Foot of mine as far,
As who goes farthest.
Id: Sc: 7. [No. 272]

That we shall die, we know; 'tis but the Time,
And drawing Days out, that Men stand upon.
And he that cuts off twenty Years of Life,
Cutts of so many Years of fearing Death.
Grant that & then is Death a Benefit.
Id: Act. 3. Sc: 2. [No. 273]

If we are mark'd to die, we are enow
To do our Country Loss; & if to live,
The fewer Men, the greater Share of Honour.
God's Will! I pray thee wish not one Man more.
Shakespear. [No. 274]

But if it be a Sin to covet Honour,
I am the most offending Soul alive.
Id: [No. 275]

Such passages continue beyond these, but for now it is enough to say that an antagonist is beginning to emerge behind all these quotations, someone of "testy" and "waspish" humor, who may make the protagonist do that he will be sorry for. The antagonist may be male, but in recalling the "father's doom" of earlier passages we must recall that Jefferson's father had died in 1754, so was no longer present, though his doom was, and recall also that explicitly gendered hatred of sinister women already drawn forth from Milton in the midst of this same context of rebellion and resentment. A further hint that the obsession with conflict is gendered may lie as well in a succeeding series of excerpts drawn from Dryden and Jonson, in which a portrait of female fortune who makes fools, not men (or who makes fools of men), is followed by more outraged pledges to pluck all into chaos, to dare challenge heaven itself.

The picture established in these two early runs of quotations emerges far more firmly in a third and chronologically slightly later set of twenty-eight excerpts that dominates a bloc of forty-four in all, whose handwriting nonetheless still dates them from before 1763.[5] This final early set takes up the same themes as before and elaborates them powerfully and without cease to the end of the series of surviving notes in Jefferson's pre-1763 handwriting. Once again, within and possibly across the works excerpted by Jefferson, the quotations as given here are probably in his original order, albeit possibly with some intervening works missing, and in all events the excerpts given here are in the order Jefferson gave them in 1768.

Julius Caesar is once again featured, but this time in the Duke of Buckingham's strident recasting of Shakespeare's play. Oppression and implicit resistance are still highest on the agenda.

> I know where I shall wear this Dagger then:
> Cassius from Bondage will deliver Cassius.
> Herein the Poor are rich, the Weak most strong;
> By this the wretched mock at base Oppression;
> The meanest are victorious o'er the mighty.
> Not Tow'rs of Stone, Nor Walls of harden'd Brass,
> Nor airless Dungeons, the poor Strength of Tyrants!
> Not all their strongest Guards, nor heaviest Chains,

Can in the least controul the mighty Spirit.
For noble Life, when weary of itself,
Has allways Power to shake it off at Pleasure,
Since I know this, know all the World besides,
That Part of Tyranny prepar'd for me,
I can & will defy.—

And so can I.
Thus ev'ry Bondman in his own Hand bears
The Pow'r to cancel his Captivity.
And why should Caesar be a Tyrant then?
Poor Man! I know he would not be a Wolf,
But that he sees the Romans are but Sheep:
He were no Lion if we were not Lambs.
Id: Sc: 5. [No. 298]

——where does Nature or the Will of Heav'n
Subject a Creature to one like itself?
Man is the only Brute enslaves his Kind.
Buck: Death of Marc: Brut: Act. 1.
Sc: 3. [No. 299]

——If hearing Lyes
With greedy Ears, & soon beleiving them;
If misinterpreting whate'er I do
And representing Things in foulest Colours,
Can be call'd wronging, who was e'er so wrong'd?
Id: Act: 4. Sc: 3. [No. 300]

To be thus enslaved, wronged, misinterpreted, is truly to be oppressed.

The nature of the implied oppressor emerges fully in the immediately ensuing and gendered series of excerpts from Thomas Otway's *The Orphan*. As the entire series makes clear, the topic is women, freedom, power, and death.

——Wed her!
No! were she all Desire could wish, as fair
As would the vainest of her Sex be thought,

With Wealth beyond what Woman's Pride could waste,
She should not cheat me of my Freedom. Marry!
When I am old & weary of the World,
I may grow desparate,
And take a Wife to mortify withal.

Otway's Orph: Act: 1. [No. 301]

——Your Sex
Was never in the Right; y'are allways false,
Or silly, ev'n your Dresses are not more
Fantastic than your Appetites; you think
Of Nothing twice: Opinion you have none.
To Day y'are nice, tomorrow not so free;
Now smile, then frown; now sorrowful, then glad;
Now pleas'd, now not; And all you know not why?
Virtue you affect, Inconstancy's your Practice;
And when your loose Desires once get Dominion,
No hungry Churl feeds coarser at a Feast;
Ev'ry rank Fool goes down.—

Id: [No. 302]

Who'd be that sordid foolish Thing call'd Man,
To cringe thus, fawn, & flatter for a Pleasure,
Which Beasts enjoy so very much above him?
The lusty Bull ranges through all the Field,
And from the Herd singling his Female out,
Enjoys her, & abandons her at Will.

Id: [No. 303]

These excerpts leave little doubt in my mind that the implied antagonist of all these impassioned early entries, entries quite uncharacteristic of the commonplace later in the 1760's and in the 1770's, is female. In the ensuing and ungendered selections, then, it must be a woman whom the protagonist of the subtextual rhetoric underlying these excerpts will not flatter or treat with politic behavior.

No Flattery, Boy! an honest Man can't live by't,
It is a little sneaking Art, which Knaves
Use to cajole & soften Fools withal.

If thou hast Flattery in thy Nature, out with't,
Or send it to a Court, for there 'twill thrive.
Id: Act. 2. [No. 304]

——shun
The Man that's singular, his Mind's unsound
His Spleen o'erweighs his Brains; but above all,
Avoid the politic, the factious Fool,
The busy, buzzing, talking, harden'd Knave,
The quaint smooth-rough, that sins against his Reason,
Call saucy loud Suspicion, public Zeal,
And Mutiny, the Dictates of his Spirit;
Be very careful how you make new Freinds.
Otw: Orph: Act: 3. [No. 305]

The final quotation from *The Orphan* removes all doubt as to the nature of the enemy:

I'd leave the World for him that hates a Woman.
Woman the Fountain of all human Fraility!
What mighty ills have not been done by Woman?
Who was't betray'd the Capitol? A Woman.
Who lost Marc Anthony the World? A Woman.
Who was the Cause of a long ten years War,
And laid at last old Troy in ashes? Woman.
Destructive, damnable, deceitful Woman!
Woman to Man first as a Blessing giv'n,
When Innocence & Love were in their Prime;
Happy a while in Paradise they lay,
But quickly Woman long'd to go astray;
Some foolish new Adventure needs must prove,
And the first devil she saw, she chang'd her Love;
To his Temptations lewdly, she inclin'd
Her Soul, & for an Apple damn'd Mankind.
Id: [No. 306]

As Nicholas Rowe's *The Fair Penitent* succeeds Otway's *Orphan*, the argument develops conclusively. The stake, as if it were not already clear, is life itself. Whether omnivorous female desire consumes men and consigns them, no longer human but mere animals, to the "herd" of exhausted lovers, or whether female hatred blocks men's ability to reproduce themselves, either way it spells the death of male humanity.

——All the Heav'n they hope for is Variety.
One Lover to another still succeeds,
Another, & another after that,
And the last Fool is welcome as the former,
'Till, having lov'd his Hour out, he gives Place
And mingles with the Herd that goes before him.
Rowe's Fair Penit: Act. 1. [No. 307]

You blast the Fair with Lies because they scorn you[,]
Hate you like Age, like Ugliness & Impotence;
Rather than make you bless'd they would die Virgi[ns,]
And stop the Propagation of Mankind.
Id: Act: 2. [No. 308]

The intensity of the rhetoric and the frequency of such quotations has now reached the point at which, even if the thoughts recorded here were not originally of the high frequency or in the order in which Jefferson preserved them in 1768—and they almost certainly were in this order and such quotations could in fact have been even more frequent in the commonplace as originally kept in the late 50's and early 60's—one might arrange them in any order and dilute them considerably and the entwined subjects of power, rebellion, evil women, and death would dominate the commonplace by their intensity alone.

As Rowe succeeded Otway, so next the Otway of *Venice Preserved* succeeds Rowe. A brief vision of a woman truly loving in spite of all the stories about their sex gives way to new railings against an ungendered but in context almost surely female antagonist. Some new hints emerge as to her character:

Can there in Women be such glorious Faith?
Sure all ill Stories of thy Sex are false!
O Woman! lovely Woman! Nature made thee

To temper Man: we had been Brutes without you:
Angels are painted fair to look like you:
There's in you all that we beleive of Heav'n,
Amazing Brightness, Purity & Truth,
Eternal joy, & everlasting Love.
Otw: Ven: preserv: Act: l. [No. 309]

Cowards are scar'd with Threatnings; Boys are whipt
Into Confessions: but a steady Mind
Acts of itself, ne'er asks the Body counsel.
Give him the Tortures! Name but such a Thing
Again, by Heav'n I'll shut these Lips for ever.
Not all your Racks, your Engines, or your Wheels,
Shall force a Groan away, that you may guess at.
Id: Act. 4. [No. 310]

——You want to lead
My Reason blindfold, like a Hamper'd Lion,
Check'd of its nobler Vigour; then when bated
Down to obedient Tameness, make it couch,
And shew strange tricks, which you call Signs of Faith.
So silly Souls are gull'd, & you get Money.
Away; no more:—
Id: Act. 5. [No. 311]

Throughout the many previous and gendered passages, it is the enslaving and deceptive as well as the insatiable character of women which has been emphasized and here the antagonist, though not explicitly gendered, is again enslaving and deceptive. Further, "Boys are whipt into confessions" and "You [who] want to lead my reason blindfold, . . . show strange tricks so silly souls are gulled, and you get Money Away; no more," raise interesting questions in this boy's and young man's commonplace. Why out of all the rich realm of English literature do such passages appeal to Thomas Jefferson at this moment? Could they be deeply autobiographical?

The suggestion that Jefferson's previous misogynistic excerpts in particular have an autobiographical resonance is reinforced by the fact that they are often being taken from far less misogynistic contexts. While William Byrd's rewriting of his excerpts often obscures their origin and so leaves uncertain the degree to which he was taking his unusually focused selection of misogynistic anecdotes out of originally less misogynistic sources, in Jefferson's case there can be little doubt. Even Milton, whose putative misogyny has been a subject of much debate, has found defenders who maintain that his Eve, for example, was a vital source of new models of admirable womanhood in the eighteenth century. But that is not how Jefferson has used the balanced Milton of *Paradise Lost*, here above, and he is soon to turn to the more mysogynistic Milton of *Samson Agonistes*, to still more powerful effect. Otway's and Rowe's fascination with the tragic and noble dimensions of womanhood, and with the deadly implications for women of male ambivalence and lust, are so well established that their plays are identified as "she-tragedies." The very speeches Jefferson excerpts here are put by these playwrights in the mouths of disillusioned men—for example Polydora, in Otway's *Orphan*, and Horatio in Rowe's *The Fair Penitent*—who fail to see the extent to which the "fall" of the specific woman to which each speaker is referring is produced by the failures of a patriarchal society and of an unforgiving male nature. Jefferson has quite simply ripped these misogynistic speeches out of context when he takes them alone from these "she-tragedies" and places them in his context of rage, struggle, and power, leaving the pained and heroic women of those plays utterly out of sight. The only conclusion must be that misogyny, rage, and power are somehow linked in his mind at this moment in his life.[6]

Jefferson's commonplace then returns briefly to the kind of ambivalence on gender and power seen earlier, and now found in a run of passages from Rowe's *Tamerlane*, Mallet's *Euridice*, Dodsley's *The Art of Charming*, and Rowe's *Lady Jane Grey*. On the one hand the enraged protagonist will *not* be forced to obey, as "I am a Man." Yet women need not be evil; "like summer storms [they] a while are cloudy. / Burst out in thunder and impeteous Show're / But straight the Sun of Beauty dawns abroad, / and all the fair Horizon is serene [*Tamerlane*, Act: 5. Sc. 1.]" (Wilson, no. 315). Women actually sorrow, like poor Euridice: "—Say now Melissa / Is there among the Daughters of Affliction / One so forlorn as poor Eurydice? [Mallet's *Euridice.* Act: 1. Sc. 1.]" (Wilson, no. 316). Yes, but women's tears are perhaps also but a stratagem: "Would Tears, my gracious Mistress, aught avail us / Methinks these aged Eyes could number Drops / With falling Clouds, or the perpetual Stream. [Ib: Sc: 4.]" (Wilson, no. 317), and no man can ever win to sympathy a woman whose "Rooted Hate is not to be removed [Id: Sc: 6.]" (Wilson, no. 318). This, the quotation continues, "was my Soul's first Aim, the towering Poi[nt] / Of all my Wishes, to prevail in this." Then the mood turns wistful once again, to the effect that external beauty in a woman is nothing compared to peace of mind and harmony within: "What is the blooming Tincture of a Skin / To Peace of Mind, to Harmony within? / What the bright Sparkling of the finest Eye / To the soft soothing of a calm Reply? / Can Comeliness of Form, or Shape, or Air, / With Comeliness of Words, or Deeds, compare? / No;—those at first th'unwary Heart may gain; / But these, these only can that Heart retain. [The Art of charming.]" (Wilson, no. 319). As in the quotation on "my Mother's Lap," is there a wish for peace behind this sentiment? But immediately thereafter, hope in an eventual, idealized beauty, presumably one possessing also inner virtue, again is followed by the prospect of rejection by someone near at hand: "The sex" were but gaudy flowers "till she [an idealized mistress] came with every Grace that Nature's Hand could give [Id: Act: 3.]" (Wilson, no. 321). Yet, immediately afterwards, "Thy narrow Soul Knows not the God-like Glory of forgiving [Id: Act. 5. Sc: 1.]" (Wilson, no. 322).

Whatever ambivalences about women exist in the transcriber's mind do not prevail in the ensuing and final quotations in this entire set, which are drawn from Milton's *Samson Agonistes*. Here, in excerpts from a tale of a strong man emasculated by a woman's wiles, the themes of gender, defeat, and ruin mingle in conclusive form. A restless, troubled introductory passage opens the series:

Retiring from the popular Noise, I seek
This unfrequented place to find some Ease,
Ease to the Body some, none to the Mind
From restless Thoughts, that like a deadly swarm
Of Hornets arm'd, no sooner found alone
But rush upon me thronging, & present
Times past, what once I was, & what am now.
Milton's Samson Agonistes. v: 16 [No. 324]

For the next fifteen entries dejection, defeat, and solitude rule, then suddenly give place to Samson's riddle, one very like that restated in our own day by Sigmund Freud: "What does woman want?"

It is not Virtue, Wisdom, Valour, Wit,
Strength, Comeliness of Shape, or amplest Merit,
That Woman's Love can win or long inherit;
But what it is, hard is to say,
Harder to hit,
(Which way soever Men refer it)
Much like thy Riddle Samson in one Day
Or sev'n, though one should musing sit.
Id: v: 1010. [No. 340]

Whatever she wants, it is woman, outwardly beautiful but inwardly foolish if not evil, who stands at the center of a contest for domestic power. The outcome of that contest will determine the very order or disorder of life itself:

Is it for that such outward Ornament
Was lavish'd on their Sex, that inward Gifts
Were left for Haste unfinished, judgment scant,
Capacity not rais'd to apprehend
Or value what is best

In Choice, but oftest to affect the Wrong?
Or was too much of Self-Love mix'd,
Of Constancy no Root infix'd,
That either they love Nothing, or not long?
    Whate'er it be to wisest Men & best
Seeming at first all-heav'nly under Virgin Vail.
Soft, modest, meek, demure,
Once join'd, the contrary she proves, a Thorn
Intestine, far within defensive Arms
A cleaving Mischeif, in his Way to Virtue
Adverse & turbulent, or by her Charms
Draws him away inslav'd
With Dotage, & his Sense deprav'd
To Folly & shameful Deeds which Ruin ends.
What Pilot so expert but needs must wreck,
Imbark'd with such a Steersmate at the Helm?
    Favour'd of Heav'n who finds
One virtuous rarely found,
That in domestic Good combines:
Happy that House! his Way to Peace is smoo[th]
But Virtue which breaks through all Opposition
And all Temptations can remove,
Most shines, & most is acceptable above.
    Therefore God's universal Law
Gave to Man despotic Power
Over his Female in due Awe,
Nor from that Right to part an Hour,
Smile she or lour:
So shall he least Confusion draw
On his whole Life, no sway'd
By female Usurpation, or dismay'd.

Id: v: 1025. [No. 341]

Two isolated clusters of three quotations each, found in isolation amidst a very long series of entries on miscellaneous topics originally recorded in 1762–1765, a bit later than the quotations discussed above (and in 1768 moved back to earlier points in his editing of the commonplace), may represent the young Jefferson's final judgment on women. They are the only opinion on the subject at this later date, by which time not only women but also power and rebellion have begun quite dramatically to recede from the pages of the commonplace, probably both in the original and in Jefferson's reconstruction of 1768. The first of these tiny clusters is from Edward Young's *Night Thoughts on Life, Death, and Immortality*, a work to which Jefferson was to return again and again in the later commonplace and in his life.[7] It begins innocuously enough with a typically romantic Youngian observation on love's pleasing anguish. But the second excerpt leaves finally no doubt that beneath feminine beauty lies a siren of death.

——Ah then, ye fair!
Be greatly cautious of your sliding hearts;
Dare not th'infectious sigh; the pleading eye,
In meek submission drest, deject, and low,
But full of tempting guile. Let not the tongue,
Prompt to deceive, with adulation smooth,
Gain on your purpos'd will. Nor in the bower,
Where woodbines flaunt, and roses shed a couch
While evening draws her crimson curtains round,
Trust your soft minutes with betraying man.
And let th'aspiring youth beware of love,
Of the smooth glance beware; for 'tis too late,
When on his heart the torrent softness pours.
Then wisdom prostrate lies; and fading fame
Dissolves in air away: while the fond soul
Is wrapt in dreams of ecstacy, and bliss;
Still paints th'illusive form; the kindling grace;
Th'inticing smile; the modest-seeming eye,
Beneath whose beauteous beams, belying heaven,
Lurk searchless cunning, cruelty and death:
And still, false-warbling in his cheated ear,
Her syren voice, enchanting draws him on,
To guileful shores, and meads of fatal joy.

Id: v. 887. [No. 284]

A final selection from Young then confirms that, for those who love women, the world is a landscape of death.

The second cluster of three, this one rather a scattered collection, occurs amidst a long and generally quite innocuous series of quotations in Greek from Euripides, all also written in 1762–1765. The first of these is conventional enough save in context:

Now the race of women by nature loves scandal; and if they get some slight handle for their gossip they exaggerate it, for they seem to take a pleasure in saying everything bad of one another.

Phoenissae v: 206. [No. 117, Tran., Wilson]

After thirteen quotations which do not speak to issues of gender, we encounter still another time and in very blunt form a wish that may be at the center of Jefferson's response to women, that men could reproduce without women:

Yea, men should have begotten children from some other source, no female race existing; thus would no evil ever have fallen on mankind.

Id: v. 573. [No. 132, Tran., Wilson]

After fourteen more unrelated entries comes a positive tirade from Euripides which, as if the point were not already abundantly clear, articulates fully the ways in which women are a threat to patriarchal power.

Great Zeus, why didst thou, to man's sorrow, put woman, evil counterfeit, to dwell where shines the sun? If thou wert minded that the human race should multiply, it was not from women they should have drawn their stock, but in thy temples they should have paid gold or iron or ponderous bronze and bought a family, each man proportioned to his offering, and so in independence dwelt, from women free. But now as soon as ever we would bring this plague into our home we bring its fortune to the ground. 'Tis clear from this how great a curse a woman is; the very father, that begot and nurtured her, to rid him of the mischief, gives her a dower and packs her off; while the husband, who takes the noxious weed into his home, fondly decks his sorry idol in fine raiment and tricks her out in robes, squandering by degrees, unhappy wight! his house's wealth. For he is in this dilemma; say his marriage has brought him good connections, he is glad then to keep the wife he loathes; or, if he gets a good wife but useless relations, he tries to stifle the bad luck with the good. But it is easiest for him who has settled in his house as wife a mere nobody. . . .

Id: v. 616. [No. 146, Tran. Wilson]

In subsequent years, from 1768 well into the 1770's, Jefferson's selections are substantially intact in their original sequence, and by then he was selecting very few passages on rebellion and fewer still on women. The latter were brief, conventionalized, and predominantly but by no means entirely negative. "Misfortune" is a she; the fates are "fatal sisters"; so are the days of life, and these are fatally deceiving. Interspersed with these are female beams of light and daughters of heaven. In the 1770's a newly married Jefferson gave Samuel Butler the last word, in a selection from *Hudibras*:

For Wedlock, without love, some say,
Is but a lock without a key.
id. part. 2. Canto 1. 321. [No. 216]

By all accounts Jefferson's was a loving marriage.

Jefferson does not offer us the help William Byrd did. He does not try to tell us why, in this case between the ages of thirteen and twenty-one, and to a sharply lessening degree thereafter, themes of power and misogyny dominated his commonplace book. But this fact has been noted by Jack McLaughlin, though its anatomy has not been as fully explored as here. In his lovely *Jefferson and Monticello: The Biography of a Builder*, McLaughlin ranges well beyond architecture. Struck by these impassioned early entries in the commonplace, he offers a suggestion as to their origin, and in so doing he extends an earlier analysis of Jefferson's youth made by Fawn Brodie more than fifteen years ago.[8] Jefferson's father, Peter Jefferson, had died in 1757, when his son was fourteen, "an age when boys struggle with issues of independence-dependence, separation from parental control, and the assertion of their maleness." His mother was left in effective control of Thomas, of his five sisters and younger brother, and of much of his father's estate. In the will she was explicitly given control of the family's new mansion, Shadwell, built under Peter Jefferson's direction in 1753–1754. From all the evidence, she assumed full control of the house and of the plantation.

The rash of quotations on power, rebellion, and hateful women—and, I add, the references to the fatally ignorant decisions of men who marry, to a father's doom, to a vain wish to lay one's head in a mother's lap yet an inability to trust, to being misunderstood, to whipped boys, to struggles over money, to a desperate need to assert manhood and independence—all date from the years that stretch from Peter Jefferson's death to Thomas Jefferson's attainment of legal independence at the age of twenty-one in April of 1764. In *theory* the earliest quotations could date a bit earlier, as Jefferson used this hand as early as 1756, but certainly most (and, under the circumstances, I should guess all) post-date his father's death and predate his majority. The suggestion is inescapable, as McLaughlin observes, that the implied antagonist of these unique tirades is Thomas Jefferson's mother, Jane Randolph Jefferson, a wealthy widow in control of her oldest son's resources but not of his youthful self-image or of his burning ambitions. McLaughlin points out that after his mother's death in 1776 Jefferson seems to have burned his correspondence with her, curiously enough just three months before he wrote the Declaration of Independence, and notes further that remaining evidence indicates that "his relationship with his mother was not a loving one." Jefferson's few surviving references to his mother are either sarcastic or cold.[9]

There is more to McLaughlin's story. The implicit and explicit injunctions in the commonplace to marry women with inward harmony, and women able to submit to man's dominion, were carried out in Jefferson's life when he married Martha Wayles. She was a modest, domestic woman who in the end proved not strong enough for the duties of household management and child-rearing. His love for her was unmistakable but she never challenged his power or shared in his political interests.[10] Jefferson explicitly encouraged both his wife and daughters to confine their interests to home and children. He also wanted them to be "fastidious about cleanliness and grooming." His advice to his eleven-year-old daughter Martha suggests that his fear of female sexuality and well-known passion for cleanliness were linked in his mind:

> Some ladies think they may under the privileges of the dishabille be loose and negligent of their dress in the morning. But be you from the moment you rise till you go to bed as cleanly and properly dressed as at the hours of dinner or tea. A lady who has been seen as a slut or a sloven in the morning, will never efface the impression she then made with all the dress and pageantry she can afterwards involve herself in.

By offering this evidence, McLaughlin is essentially confirming an assessment of Jefferson's psychosexual makeup put forward by Winthrop Jordan twenty years earlier: "Intimate emotional engagement with women seemed to represent for him a gateway into a dangerous, potentially explosive world which threatened revolution against the discipline of his higher self. As Jefferson matured, he seems to have mitigated this inner tension imputing potential explosiveness to the opposite sex."[11]

Peculiarly enough McLaughlin leaves out the last step in the chain of evidence that articulates Jefferson's reaction to women. In 1794, by this time long a widower and one who was never to remarry, Thomas Jefferson began the project that was to be the ultimate expression of his life. He began rebuilding Monticello into the house that now exists. To walk through the house is to see that it expresses the man in many ways. It is above all the pavilion of the aristocrat as enlightened and democratic intellectual. Modelled on the richly modest town mansions of liberal French aristocrats, it is the theater of such an aristocrat's inventive and discursive mind. Yet it also contains subtle reminders—as in the relics of the Lewis and Clark expedition scattered about the entrance hall—of his geopolitical power. In order to be these things, the house must pretend that it is not what Jefferson also wanted it to be, an imposing three-story Palladian brick mansion, a "power-house," high on a hill, the sort of house every Virginia gentleman wanted. Simultaneously the house had to pretend not to be what Jefferson grudgingly had to admit it must also be, namely a house large enough to have room for his daughters, grandchildren, and other family and retainers. It "pretends" it is neither a powerhouse nor a large family residence by such devices as carrying the windows on the east front one-and-a-half stories almost in a single sweep, echoing the tall single windows on the west front which illuminated the main floor alone. These east front windows in fact lighted both the first and second story rooms but made the house appear as if it were only a one-story pavilion. To maintain the illusion, other second floor rooms were lighted by tiny windows hidden under the eaves as part of the south pediment. The result is that in the cramped family rooms upstairs some windows rise from the floor only to the chest while others are miniscule. The house "pretends" it is but a single floor in another vital respect, by suppressing the stairways into what are virtually narrow, dark, dangerous ladders hidden behind the doors to the halls on the main floor. A dark, small, parlor-like space, really part of the library, down a hall to the left of the front entrance, is the only family space on this main floor and it is well hidden. No visitor need know that the house is anything but a single man's pavilion of himself. Family, and with it women, are profoundly suppressed.[12]

If you visit, you will be told that Jefferson's favorite daughter Martha Jefferson Randolph lived in the house and helped him entertain here. But Martha saw the house and her father's use of it for what they were, a form of self-display. As she wrote to him of one of her visits there:

> I never had the pleasure of passing one sociable moment with you.

Always in a crowd, taken from every useful and pleasing duty to be worried with a multiplicity of disagreeable ones, which the entertaining of such crowds of company subjects one to in the country.

In reply, he pleaded duty to "the present manners and uses of our country."[13] But his meticulously constructed and crushingly expensive house was his role and his self displayed. Just as in "The Female Creed" William Byrd appropriated the enlightenment, leaving no role in it for women, so family had no visible role in Jefferson's fashionable and enlightened theater of himself. Perhaps if he had had a son? But he did not. Nor did he marry again and try. For much of his life he lived without a mate, but as a result he failed to reproduce himself, and his house was a house of himself only.

Vanitys, there is none more ridiculous than when we
make ostentation of our Exploits with the women. Whereas
Supposeing every word we said of our might in that particular
were true, there's hardly a Brute in the Creation but is able to
perform oftener with his Female than we can do, nay a poor
Sparrow or even a diminutive Fly coud they speak as well as
they coud in Æsops time, might call the ablest of our Boasters
a Fumbler. The Emperor Proculus pretended that he had laid with
an Hundred Sarmatian Women, which he had taken in the wars,
in less than a Fortnight. mighty Feats for an Emperour to
glory in, when a Ram will tup that Number of Ewes in one
night & impregnate them all! Crusius tells us a Story that a
Strong Servant in his neighbourhood, got ten wenches with
child in one night. This indeed was doing business, and no
man upon Record ever did more, except Hercules himself, who
is famed for haveing got 50 boys in one night upon the Bodys of 50 Athenian Damsels, and if this was true, it was
the greatest of all his atcheivements. The Spaniards are
famous for doing handsome things with the Women as appears
by the Complaint of a Catalonian Lady exhibited against her
Husband. She fell down at the Kings feet & implord his Protection. The good King askt her what might be her Grievance.
Lord Sire said she, I am a dead Woman unless your Majesty
protect me from a hard hearted Husband. What dos he do to
you madam reply'd the King? alas Sire said she, he dos more
to me than any Husband in all Spain dos to his Wife, He is
impertinent at least ten times every night. By St Jago answerd the King if this be true he deserves to dye, for he will
make every other Woman in my Dominions despise her Husband.
However he mitigated his punishment & made him give Security for his good behaviour, and strictly enjoind him not to assault
the complainant more than 6 times a night for the future.

When the ancients painted Venus, they generally shewd Mercury in some part of the Picture, which carry'd this notable instruction,
that we shoud always let Reason have some share in our Love, to direct
and keep it within Bounds, least what is intended by Providence for our hap-

83

1. Page 83 of William Byrd's commonplace book. Original in and photo courtesy of the Virginia Historical Society.

2. Portrait of William Byrd circa 1715–1725. In the possession of and photo courtesy of the Virginia Historical Society.

35

Would thunder in my Ears: ——

B: 10. l: 769.

—— imagin'd wise,
Constant, mature, proof against all Assaults:
And understood not all was but a Shew,
Rather than solid Virtue; all but a Rib,
Crooked by Nature, bent (as now appears)
More to the Part sinister from me drawn;
Well if thrown out, as supernumerary
To my just Number found! — O! why did Go
Creator wise! that peopl'd highest Heav'n
With Spirits masculine, create at last
This Novelty on Earth, this fair Defect
Of Nature? And not fill the World at once
With Men, as Angels, without feminine?
Or find some other Way to generate
Mankind? This Mischeif had not then befall
And more that shall befal: innumerable
Disturbances on Earth through female Snares,
And straight Conjunction with this Sex! ——

3. Page 35 of Thomas Jefferson's commonplace book. Photo courtesy of the Library of Congress.

4. Portrait of Thomas Jefferson. By an unknown artist. From the collections of and photo courtesy of the Maryland Historical Society.

5. Aerial view of Monticello. Photo courtesy of Colonial Williamsburg, Inc.

6. Aerial view of Monticello. Original loaned from Monticello, Thomas Jefferson Memorial Foundation, Inc.

7. West portico, Monticello. Photo by Gerald Kling.

8. Entrance hall, Monticello. Photo courtesy of Monticello, Thomas Jefferson Memorial Foundation, Inc.

9. East portico, Monticello. Photo courtesy of Monticello, Thomas Jefferson Memorial Foundation, Inc., James T. Thatch.

10. Detail of south pediment and balustrade, Monticello. Photo courtesy of Colonial Williamsburg, Inc.

11. Upstairs window, Monticello. Original loaned from Monticello, Thomas Jefferson Memorial Foundation, Inc.

12. Stairway, Monticello. Photo courtesy of Colonial Williamsburg, Inc.

CHAPTER 4

ON THE SOURCES OF PATRIARCHAL RAGE

JEFFERSON'S commonplace, with its rampant misogyny and impassioned associations of women with male extinction, was, like Byrd's, a confessional text. Just as Byrd was confessing his despair at his failure perhaps to control his own household and certainly to use younger women to gain access to patriarchal resources, so Jefferson was confessing a frustration with and hatred of his mother's control of similar resources. In both cases, and most prominently Jefferson's, rage was the result. Byrd's confession arose from a lifetime of failure to exercise his power over women and increase his power through them, and Jefferson's came as he first encountered this problem. Both Byrd's and Jefferson's confessions were followed by later distancing from and caution with women; both later married meek women, and when Jefferson's wife died he never remarried. Foucault was certainly right when he said that in the eighteenth century the literature of sexuality was inherently confessional.[1]

At this point I have a confession to make. It is that I find these outbursts disturbing. I don't have a scholarly category for my dismay, or a way to capture the unique intensity of what these two men are saying in their sub-rhetorical ways. To chop up the quotations they use, as I have done here, is to miss the terrible depth of their fear and of their implicit will and of their hatred. The effect is in the total assembly each man makes. They must be read whole. Feminist theory tells us that all of this is no surprise, but the surprise is, first of all, in the reading, in the cumulative power of these horrifying assemblages. They are disguised emotion, typical of the eighteenth century; Byrd and Jefferson knew that by using others' words and often literary words in a book that is nominally a superficial assembly of clever rhetorical expressions of the conventional, they could pretend not to be saying what they really were. Yet these intense concentrations of misogyny, taken out of the vast universe of available rhetorics, do not lie. With both, but particularly with Jefferson, these fragments of thought acquire a greater power by being out of their original and often far more balanced contexts, out of their role as mere anecdote or as speeches in a fictionalized drama, and by being presented here naked as fact in relentless sequence. The message becomes revealing, powerful, and full of fear and hatred. The theory of patriarchy, and as we shall see patriarchy is what is at stake here, is one thing; its practice in this bitter form is quite another.

While I may seem an apologist for men in what follows here, I would like it to be remembered that I am not. Something this strong cannot be explained away. As I read over the analysis and categorization that follows, I am disappointed that it does not capture the power of the outbursts in these commonplaces. Analysis defeats the very effort to show this; I do not know otherwise how to deal with them, however, and the actual practice (must I call it praxis?) of patriarchy as they reveal it is surely as important a subject of analysis as all the theories about patriarchy we already have. So I must go on to try to analyze what is happening here.

Let me emphasize first of all that these two confessions *are* private distillations of misogyny. As such, it seems to me, they are much more powerful than public misogyny. The fashionable and condescending witticisms about women found in the English press, the caustic epigrams and poems in English compendia, in and of themselves or as reprinted in the Virginia *Gazette*, represent a strain of misogyny-for-show that was itself both a sign and a buttress of patriarchal fear and power. In these, an implicit threat was made explicit. But the threat was also witty, public, a distanced pose which seemed to say, "Now I am going to do the frail-is-woman number." A silent subtext then said, "my misogyny is real but also only a pose, a sally in the wars of the sexes, in which women give as good as they get." To Byrd's and Jefferson's relentlessly assembled fear and hatred of women there is virtually no such subtext. This is private rage, not public play.[2]

What is the structure of Thomas Jefferson's implicit misogyny, in relation to that of William Byrd? With Thomas Jefferson as with William Byrd the brief episode of agonized entries about women and power found in the man's commonplace stands as the confessional turning point of a life characterized at first by problematic and later by carefully delimited and controlled relationships with women. So it is vital to ask what is the nature of the gendered otherness that Jefferson here assigns to women as it compares to that constructed by his Virginia predecessor.

In my eyes they are very similar. Jefferson's is a more obviously gendered construction of women than Byrd's, but both are gendered. That is, Jefferson makes no claims to anatomical comparisons and so invokes virtually no "objective" distinctions between men and women. Even female beauty is not truly anatomical; beyond lovely skin and hair, beauty is found in manner and in behavior, whether this be deceptive or genuine. So what is at stake here is deanatomized gender traits, intangibles of inner nature and character. Yet this is also true of William Byrd once he dismisses anatomical and reproductive superiority and female desire becomes his whole agenda. Whether or not they are anatomical in nature, however, for both men intangible female traits are constructions equally as permanent and objective as anatomy is thought to be. Jefferson admits only rare exceptions and Byrd virtually none to the fact that women "are" as these quotations construct them, irrespective of context, time, or space.

Female sexual desire ranks very high in each man's catalog of fear. True, with Jefferson desire is sometimes disembodied or scarcely named. This is because Jefferson is far more concerned with the way women's outer beauty masks purported treacherousness in all areas, not just the sexual. Man is ever "weak against the charm of beauty's powerful glance," against women's "too much of ornament, . . . outward Show elaborate." "What admirest thou," the poet asks himself, "what transports thee so? An Outside? Fair no Doubt and worthy well thy . . . Love, [but] Not thy Subjection." But beneath the outward show of woman, female sexual appetites and "loose Desires" lurk in Jefferson's just as in Byrd's passages: ". . . when your loose Desires once get Dominion, No hungry churl feeds coarser at a Feast; Every Rank Fool goes down." Women offer their "lewdness" and in return, overwhelming man's feebler desire, possess his soul [no. 306, Wilson]. In the passages from Young's *Night Thoughts* the anatomical landscape of desire, the female body and its beauties, becomes a landscape of death for men, the love feast, a feast of death.

——Ah then, ye fair!
Be greatly cautious of your sliding hearts;
Dare not th'infectious sigh; the pleading eye,
In meek submission drest, deject, and low,
But full of tempting guile. Let not the tongue,
Prompt to deceive, with adulation smooth,
Gain on your purpos'd will. Nor in the bower,
Where woodbines flaunt, and roses shed a couch
While evening draws her crimson curtains round,
Trust your soft minutes with betraying man.
And let th'aspiring youth beware of love,
Of the smooth glance beware; for 'tis too late,
When on his heart the torrent softness pours.
Then wisdom prostrate lies; and fading fame
Dissolves in air away: while the fond soul
Is wrapt in dreams of ecstacy, and bliss;
Still paints th'illusive form; the kindling grace;
Th'inticing smile; the modest-seeming eye,

> Beneath whose beauteous beams, belying heaven,
> Lurk searchless cunning, cruelty and death:
> And still, false-warbling in his cheated ear,
> Her syren voice, enchanting draws him on,
> To guileful shores, and meads of fatal joy.
> Id: v. 887. [No. 284]

There are some significant differences in the two men's views as embodied in the subtextual rhetoric each employs in linking his carefully selected entries. Jefferson is far more ambivalent about women than his predecessor. He longs to lay his head in his mother's lap. He dreams of a woman who can be an exception to the very rules he is posing:

> Can there in Women be such glorious Faith?
> Sure all ill Stories of thy Sex are false!
> O Woman! lovely Woman! Nature made thee
> To temper Man: we had been Brutes without you:
> Angels are painted fair to look like you:
> There's in you all that we beleive of Heav'n,
> Amazing Brightness, Purity & Truth,
> Eternal joy, & everlasting Love.
> Otw: Ven: preserv: Act: 1. [No. 309]

After his outburst of frustration a more cynical Byrd makes a cold and polite marriage, while after his own rage Jefferson is to marry and within his limits genuinely to love a woman who seems to fulfill his prophecy of a "good" woman. And, as noted, even at his worst, for Jefferson the issue is one not only of an annihilating female sexuality but also of a threat to manhood construed as domestic and political power, independence, and control. He is focussed on female desire, but not as obsessively as Byrd. Perhaps the difference in these two constructions is the difference between a middle-aged man and an adolescent boy. Byrd has substantially abandoned his dream of power, has experienced a lifetime of failures with women, has no male heir, and has begun to wonder if even his sexual and reproductive powers still stand between himself and death. Hence, his raw sexuality and his desperation. Jefferson on the other hand, while he responds repeatedly to the threat of sexual annihilation, *is* much more concerned with masculinity as domestic rather than as sexual power. A woman, his mother, stands between him and his first exercises of masculinity as control. Masculinity as sexuality is also on the agenda but at this stage power is equally or primarily a domestic political issue.

> Her rooted Hate is not to be remov'd.
> And 'twas my Soul's first Aim, the towering Poi[nt]
> Of all my Wishes, to prevail in this.
>
> Id: Sc: 6. [No. 318]

> Therefore God's universal Law
> Gave to Man despotic Power
> Over his Female in due Awe,
> Nor from that Right to part an Hour,
> Smile she or lour:
> So shall he least Confusion draw
> On his whole Life, no sway'd
> By female Usurpation, or dismay'd.
>
> Id: v: 1025. [No. 341]

Despite these differences, there remain questions about Jefferson's construction of women and sexuality; they arise not only from the very real sexual terror explicit in some of the quotations in his commonplace but also from his actions once his need for power was met. Once his wife died, he did not remarry. The fact of his advice to his daughter to stay clean and not be a slut, and his construction of a pavilion of the self visibly without place for family or for significant women, leave us wondering whether his agenda of sexual as well as political fear of women did not triumph even over his fully realized domestic and political power.

I would argue that in the end it is impossible to distinguish between the sexual and nonsexual in either William Byrd's or in Thomas Jefferson's construction of women. What strikes me on reading the latter's commonplace book is that sexual desire as the center of an all-consuming female power, and the wider female threat to male reproduction and control of resources, resonate almost equally in Jefferson's mind, as they perhaps did ever after. He sees what William Byrd hints at in the end of his rhapsody of anecdotes about female desire: that in the end either the triumph of female sexuality or the female usurpation of male control over the household come to much the same thing; death and "disorder." Raw promiscuous sexuality and the usurpation of male control over resources together constitute a female otherness whose name is chaos.

Once join'd, the contrary she proves, a Thorn
Intestine, far within defensive Arms
A cleaving Mischeif, in his Way to Virtue
Adverse & turbulent, or by her Charms
Draws him away inslav'd
With Dotage, & his Sense depray'd
To Folly & shameful Deeds which Ruin ends. . . .
Id: v: 1025. [No. 341]

Creator wise! that Peopl'd highest Heav'n
With Spirits masculine, create at last
This Novelty on Earth, this fair Defect
Of Nature? And not fill the World at once
With Men, as Angels, without feminine?
Or find some other Way to generate
Mankind? This Mischeif had not then befall['n,]
And more that shall befal: innumerable
Disturbances on Earth through female Snares,
And straight Conjunction with this Sex!——
[Id: 1: 881] [No. 241]

For Jefferson the bottom line—if I may use an economist's metaphor for a man who went bankrupt—is exactly the same as the top and bottom lines of William Byrd's tirade: men cannot reproduce themselves without women, yet when men seek to make themselves immortal women usurp men's desire into death and male power and order into disorder. Jefferson returns again and again to the very wish implicit in the opening of Byrd's tirade, that men could reproduce entirely without women. At least one of his references borders on the genocidal [no. 132, Wilson]. Others leave no doubt that in successful male reproduction and control, without women if necessary, lie the futures of the home, or house, in short of patriarchy [no. 146; no. 308, Wilson]. Patriarchy, defined as sexuality limited by men, households controlled by men and successful male reproduction, and a term actually used by William Byrd and directly implied by Thomas Jefferson, is the opposite of chaos.

How seriously did Thomas Jefferson take the *bricolage* in his commonplace? Three quotations from Nicholas Rowe, found quite near each other in his commonplace, summarize for me the power of Jefferson's will at this deeply disturbed movement, as he assembles the otherness of women into an essay which, like Byrd's, implies that men must dominate or die.

> Rather than make you bless'd they would die Virgi[ns,]
> And stop the Propagation of Mankind.
>
> Id: Act: 2. [No. 308]

> Yet ere thou rashly urge my Rage too far,
> I warn thee to take Heed; I am a Man,
> And have the Frailties common to Man's Nature;
> The fiery Seeds of Wrath are in my Temper,
> And may be blown up to so fierce a Blaze
> As Wisdom cannot rule. Know, thou hast touch'd me
> Ev'n in the nicest, tenderest Part, my Honour.
> My Honour! which, like Pow'r, disdains being question'd;
>
> Id: Act: 4. Sc: 1. [No. 314]

> ——Thy narrow Soul
> Knows not the God-like Glory of forgiving:
> Nor can thy cold, thy ruthless Heart conceive,

How large the Power, how fix'd the Empire is,
Which Benefits confer on generous Minds:. . .
Id: Act. 5. Sc: 1. [No. 322]

So in most respects Byrd and Jefferson share a common commonplace chamber of horrors where gender is concerned. Power, sex, love, death, and chaos; it sounds positively Wagnerian. Why do these two men invoke such powerful images? Why soak in them as a true Wagnerian does? Why is love's death a sign of female evil; why is love itself and the world's *untergang* not the lovers' mutual *götterdammerung* as in Wagner, but a gendered crime? What are the relative roles of fear and rage in the two men's exhaustive categorizations of female sins? Fear is readily apparent everywhere, sexual fear, fear of rejection, fear of the denial of vital resources patriarchs need. Most of all, there is a brittle fear of the reversal of the flow of anatomical, sexual, and possessive energy, as if that energy might suddenly cease to flow from men to women and flood from women to men. It reads as if patriarchy is in imminent danger of becoming matriarchy. Whence the fear of such a sudden and terrifying reversal? Rage is present as well, however. It lies beneath the surface of Byrd's defeated and supercilious remarks on sexuality while the literal fury of a man scorned pours out in his commentary on his letters to the purportedly dishonorable and promiscuous "Charmante."[3] With Jefferson the rage is palpable and all-consuming.

How commonplace was this vision? What does it mean? On one level it is straight Foucault; by the eighteenth century sexuality is power is sexuality. On the same level on a parallel track, it is straight patriarchy, and the feminist writers are, it seems to me, more to the point than Foucault; for what is synonymous with sexuality here is not a generalized power which is simply in "the order of things." Rather, what is being threatened by women and reasserted by men is the sexuality and power of dominant patriarchs. These men are also the simultaneous constructors of a wider but still specific class-based hegemony structured around class and race as well as gender. Sexuality, these hegemons' domestic power, and their vision of the order of things politically—their whole ability to command reality—are what are at stake here.[4] Deeper still, however, it is not exactly a male *ideology* we see embodied in these quotations. Rather, it is a momentary assemblage of culture in response to specific and immediate private occasions on which these two men were threatened by women with very substantial actual power. I question whether in strict form there was such a thing as a male ideology; culture appears here as a series of selective appropriations/syntheses/enactments, of which we have just seen two. Perhaps none of these statements is surprising but their implications bear discussion.

Whether right or wrong, then, Foucault's work on sexuality and power seems to me too general to describe what is going on in these commonplaces. True, to William Byrd sexuality is power in its ultimate form, literally the power not only over the reproduction but over the life and death of the male subject. The same is true of Jefferson. But in both men the power is male power; power is gendered so that life and legitimate power are male, death and illegitimate power female. This is probably why Byrd is so troubled by female reproductive power, which itself can only seem to him a usurpation of the essential maleness of power. How can the sex most responsible for reproduction be the same whose uncontrolled desires for sex and power annihilate men, making male reproduction difficult or impossible? He and Jefferson solve this dilemma by making male replication the central form of reproduction and women simply a necessary evil, and a necessary risk of death and disorder, which men must run as they replicate themselves and their power.

This construction points up in turn the essentially domestic and patriarchal context within which both men's subtextual rhetoric occurs. That is, while women are the antithesis of ordering male power in general, and represent disordered chaos, entropy, and death, in fact the discourse is implicitly set within the framework of domestic patriarchy. Men need not only to have sex, but to have wives, in order to replicate themselves in sons who will continue their specific lines. Jefferson makes this most explicit in a series of selections where it is clearly wives who usurp power within marriage and so bring on ruin. Yet one can as easily turn this limiting frame inside out by noting that to these men domestic disorder, and the failure to become immortal by continuing their lines, *was* in effect synonymous with a universe of chaos and entropy. Thereby, patriarchy becomes both a domestic construct and a cosmology. Foucault casts his net too widely to help us understand what these men are doing.

Women could hardly be more other than in this construction of them. But what is the nature of the construction itself? Is it best called "ideology"? Does it function as repressively as ideology can? Yes and no. No, and yes. The only other detailed exploration I know of, of male categories of power in pre-revolutionary America, is contained in Ann Kibbey's *The Interpretation of Material Shapes in Puritanism.* For her, there seem to have been constantly maintained (though at the same time somewhat open-ended) mental categories and rhetorical strategies by which Puritans not only subordinated but victimized women, Native Americans, and Catholics alike.[5] I have to say that I do not see quite so essentialist an ideology in these two secular gentlemen's commonplaces from the eighteenth century.[6] Instead, I see a rather different process. At its inception stand specific women successfully exercising power over men. In William Byrd's case his first wife had successfully usurped domestic control from her correspondingly desperate and angry husband, while before and after Lucy a continuing series of young ladies who held the keys to his political advancement, culminating in Charmante, had used a woman's moment of greatest power, courtship, to judge Byrd and reject him as inadequate. Byrd tells us the immediate occasion of his tirade by inserting his letters to Charmante and railing at her for his failure. In Jefferson's case it seems inescapable that a powerful widow, his mother, is provoking his equally unique cascade of quotations constructing female tyranny and usurpation. In both men's cases, the women who enraged them had a very specific form of power, namely control over property. They controlled servants, dowries, and inheritances, patriarchal resources these men needed to realize their image of themselves. Around these defeats by women these two men assembled, from the vast reserves of eighteenth-century culture, from anatomical guides and books of classical epigrams, from Milton and Otway, from Young and Euripides, two nightmare visions of women as other, as chaos. When the occasion had passed and the defeats were absorbed or substantially overcome, each man's commonplace returned to neutral subjects. In Byrd's case there were virtually no further nasty epigrams on women and in Jefferson's very few. What had happened was not so much "ideology" as a momentary assemblage of culture into a nightmare vision of gendered otherness in the face of domestic defeats by powerful women.

This fact has several implications that I find fruitful in thinking about the nature of gender in eighteenth-century patriarchal contexts. For one thing, it restores some agency to women. Women are not, as in Kibbey, the passive victims of a ready-made and constantly assembled construction of the world that renders them *all* victims. Instead, women are using the leverages that a generally repressive social system gave them, using occasions of real female power, namely courtship and widowhood, to seize and hold power over resources and so over their futures. They are successfully defending this power and these resources against willful patriarchs and would-be patriarchs whose only consolation for the decisive frustration of their plans for power is to enter a series of nasty quotations in their commonplaces. Female power evokes male response. It is fulfilled, actualized power. The "ideology" we see assembled here is the enactment of defeated men. Precisely because the primary arena of patriarchal issues is domestic, because on this stage eligible young ladies and wealthy widows, not to mention wives who are mistresses of domestic servants, as in Lucy Byrd's case, have accepted moments of power, patriarchy, as it was found in William Byrd and in Thomas Jefferson, as an exaggerated set of male expectations, was doomed continually to such defeats. What we see assembled, then, is the frustration, rage, and misery of the losers. Perhaps patriarchy can most accurately be measured by this rage.

I do not want to take this approach too far, but only to see where it goes. One reason such nightmarish assemblies of gendered rage are few, in these and in other such books, may be that Byrd, Thomas Jefferson, and other patriarchs generally won their domestic battles. But it could equally well be that they and others like them often absorbed their defeats more gracefully, or that few men had the passionate urgings for total domestic power and inability to control their rage at failure which William Byrd and Thomas Jefferson show. I shall return to this latter theme in a moment, but somewhere in this realm of contradictory possibilities lies nonetheless the fact that male rage assembled as a nightmare vision was rare, occurring only once in each of these two commonplaces and, as we shall see, not at all in many others. What women had to face was a threatening psychosocial system, yes, and a threat that a horrendous "ideology-by-*bricolage*" would be temporarily assembled against them. They also faced the continual presence on the cultural shelf, as it were, of the bits and pieces of that potential ideology in the form of excerpts from classical authors, Milton, Otway, Young, and others. Some of these appeared, digested, in the public prints. But it seems possible that they did not face the nightmare constantly assembled in the form of a fully articulated repressive ideology, or indeed assembled at all save in rare instances and then mostly when they had defeated and enraged men.

Is this much help? It means that patriarchal ideology in its most intense form was like the Israeli atom bomb, which was once said to consist of parts on a shelf somewhere. Was it less threatening because the bomb consisted of disassembled parts on the shelf, when those parts could be united momentarily to work their devastation? Yet the analogy is not accurate. It might be more appropriate to ask which Israeli government would actually have used the bomb and under what circumstances. Perhaps only once defeat was otherwise inevitable. Even then, the analogy breaks down, because the cultural "bomb" assembled by William Byrd and Thomas Jefferson was assembled after their defeat and exploded in silence. Even here, I do not wish to whitewash patriarchy or at any rate not these two patriarchs. Both sought and subordinated submissive wives and in later years both avoided intimacy, Byrd with his second wife and Jefferson by not taking a second wife. So I must seek the assistance of feminist scholars in explaining what it may mean, that in each man's writings the nightmare of patriarchal ideology was assembled but once, briefly, in defeat. It is something we need to discuss.

Here, Lynn Hunt seems to offer some help. As she says, "The point of doing history with a focus on gender . . . is to show that the male subject is not a solid, unified, enduring, take-it-for-granted subject . . . but was instead itself under enormous pressure and anxiety in the eighteenth century." That is what I see happening here. I see men caught between the exaggerated imperatives of domestic patriarchy as they constructed it—that they must control sexuality and indeed all things in their households—and the fact that both in and out of households women had substantial power. The origins of this same ambivalence can be seen in early sixteenth-century Europe, when authorities eager to keep order within families created a patriarchal ideal which made each man the little God, or Christ, of his family. The very state that spoke glowingly of the unlimited nature of each patriarch's grip over his family then proceeded in its legal, social, and religious capacities itself to exercise or by law or recognized custom to limit that very power. In actual fact it was often not the father but the state or his wife and children themselves who had power within the family. Thus, in Germany, fathers were given the right to grant or withhold permission before daughters could marry, *unless the daughter was over twenty-one*! Men were told that within the family they were little gods while in practice they were sometimes very little ones indeed.[7]

By the seventeenth century, in England, gentlemen seem to have taken the theory of patriarchy's total power very much to heart, but they still struggled to deal with its very real ambivalences in custom and in law. The Earl of Halifax's advice to his daughter, found in Byrd's library, is a case in point. He tells his daughter to choose a husband carefully, as that man will be her master ever after. His friends must become her friends, etc., etc. *Then* he tells her that she will, however, be mistress of the narrowly domestic functions of the household, of its efficient running, and of its servants. Then he implies strongly that all of these powers are in turn subject to her husband's oversight. Well, is this patriarch all-powerful or is he not? Halifax cannot seem to decide. The male subject can be rejected as a suitor, his wife has domestic rights and powers as mistress of the household, and, Halifax could have added, his widow may become the effective master of much of his estate and of his minor children if he dies. Yet this does not excuse him from the general injunction Halifax is preaching even to his daughter, that in fact the male head of household must be master of all.[8]

What William Byrd and Thomas Jefferson may show us is that, under the expectations of "patriarchy" as a loose sort of ideology or generalized injunction, the male subject had a hard time knowing what he *could* do. Men were expected to exercise total control within the domestic environment, as miniature models both of the deity and of the modern state; their very masculinity and larger social power required that they succeed at this task! But they were left to improvise in real situations where such total power was simply not theirs. In this contradictory context two patriarchs, Byrd and Jefferson, turned their defeats and frustrations into the worst nightmare their culture could assemble. Patriarchy could be a prison for the patriarchs as well as for their women. Their rage was generated as much by the imperatives that drove them as by the *de facto* power of the women who stood in their way.

Patriarchy as an ideology was supposedly on the wane. By 1690 it was no longer accepted as a model that justified monarchical absolutism in the state. By the mid-eighteenth century it had become fashionable for fathers to be not patriarchal but paternal, sensitive to the needs of their families and in sympathy with them.[9] But if Byrd and Jefferson are any indication, in private both the imperatives and the frustrations of patriarchy survived alongside the increasingly sentimentalized family relationships of a new age.

But was it simply the generalized injunctions of seventeenth and eighteenth-century patriarchy, or something more local, more specific that generated the rage we see here? The truth is that what we are talking about here may not be eighteenth-century patriarchy but rather the narrow, peculiar, and brittle version of it which emerged in Virginia, and within this context about two of that Virginia patriarchy's most compulsive practitioners. Jan Gilliam, of Colonial Williamsburg, and I are now editing the Byrd commonplace for publication. My co-editor and I have by now read fifty seventeenth- and eighteenth-century commonplace books by gentlemen living in England, New England, and Virginia. Few contain even scattered misogynistic references. None shows a tirade of male rage of the sort found in the two considered here. Not even in Virginia.[10]

So far, then, only the private commonplace utterances of William Byrd and Thomas Jefferson, the two great mythmakers of the Virginia gentry, assemble women in such a nightmarish fashion as the chaotic and reciprocal other of patriarchal power. I would suggest that in such a case what we may have here, in these

Virginia commonplace books, is a case study in the gendering of power by the leading mythmakers of a class whose power was particularly fragile and which accordingly was intensely involved in the process of constructing itself. For complex reasons, in such men as Byrd and Jefferson the vulnerabilities and driven need of that act of construction were more intensely felt, and so rose fully to the surface. In their more public utterances, these pressures emerged as successful myth-making; and in their private writings, their commonplace books, surfaced as a gendered paranoia. Their commonplaces thus offer a rare, explicit study in the willfulness required to maintain what proved to be a thin and brittle hegemony, a hegemony at once under pressure from all sides and yet because of the very vivacity by which it was maintained, among others by such men as Byrd and Jefferson, a brilliantly successful one. For other Virginia gentlemen, the commonplace, with its universal rules of variety and detachment, entailed forbidding inhibitions against emotional outbursts of this sort. Only in such driven men as Byrd and Jefferson do the pressures all members of their class shared to varying degrees, emerge, shattering temporarily the genteel surface of the genre. In sum, what we may have here is the behavior of two unusually vulnerable and unusually successful mythologizing patriachs, who expressed to a higher degree, in public *and in private*, as myth and as terror, the forces acting on their vulnerable class as a whole.

The story is too long to tell in detail, but basically a self-conscious gentry achieved *de facto* hegemony quite late in Virginia's history. It was at least thirty years after Bacon's Rebellion, which took place in 1676, that Virginia gentlemen could describe themselves as the masters of a stable and predictable social scene. Even then, in 1706, it was not much of a scene. William Byrd, who had returned from his first stay in London a year earlier to assume his inherited estates in Virginia, referred to life there as "being buried alive," and to the country itself as "this silent land." What noise there was was not exactly complimentary to the gentry.

Their social credentials had been in question ever since Nathaniel Bacon and his ruffian followers had exposed the presumed gentry's vile extractions, low educations, and grasping greed. Now, a generation later, a few of the younger planters had acquired brief local pedigrees, older wealth, and English manners. But there were still not enough of this sort to prevent one English governor, in 1711, from calling the members of the House of Burgesses a "mean," meaning low and clumsy, lot. As late as 1726, William Byrd returned one last time from London and stayed on the scene as one of the mythologizers of the *next* generation's gentility only because he could never gain recognition as a significant figure in England.[11]

It is hard to overestimate the contempt their English superiors had for these mere tobacco planters and erstwhile traders. Only quite late, after 1720 or 1730, did enough of them begin to cut an impressive and powerful enough figure to command respect from their English governors. Recent studies show that it was not until the 1740's and 50's that they were able to build the great brick mansion houses that to us typify this gentry. No sooner had they done so than many of them nearly went bankrupt, and had to "borrow" illegally from the public treasury to avoid impoverishment and loss of power. At this very moment their hegemony once again came into question from beneath, first by the Baptists, then by the generalized popular discontent and desires for participation aroused by the American Revolution, and then by increasing pressure against the very slavery that had established their wealth and unique control. Jefferson became *this* generation's adapter of the myth of gentility to Virginia conditions by intellectualizing and democratizing its image while preserving the essence of its power for at least a generation longer than it had any right to.

In this dynamic and insecure context, William Byrd and Thomas Jefferson emerge as remarkably similar figures, more than a generation apart in time. (Byrd died in 1744, the year after

Jefferson was born.) This similarity is something Jefferson may have understood, as he purchased books from Byrd's famous library when it came up for sale and he helped preserve the manuscripts in which Byrd had created and adjusted the initial myths of their class. Both men constantly looked over their shoulders at Europe as they tried to establish the superior rather than inferior *American* gentility and creativeness of their class.

When Byrd wrote to a titled English friend that patriarchal mastery in Virginia had so uniquely free a scope that the master of a plantation household was truly a first mover, akin to God, he also extolled the simplicity and honesty of what he called this American "Eden," thereby raising his role from that of shepherd in a European pastorale to that of the ultimate and originally virtuous patriarch, Adam. In his later *History of the [Dividing] Line [Between Virginia and North Carolina]*, Byrd raised new world events into the context of old world erudition, while suggesting that Virginia gentlemen like himself, who helped run that dividing line, were superior because they could lead rough frontiersmen who otherwise would not brook restraint. The vulnerabilities of his class to mockery from above, from Europe, and from below, from the free American yeomanry, are painfully evident in Byrd's *History* but are also beautifully sublimated into his myth of a local gentry superior because of its greater flexibility as well as because of its intensive control. As if to betray his lack of faith in the former claim, he commissioned one of the first of the many grand and intimidating mansions the Virginia gentry were to build in subsequent decades. He seemed by this act to be saying that in truth even an accommodating gentry could not succeed in keeping control in Virginia unless they also matched European splendor and thereby intimidated the American masses. Byrd simultaneously set about importing obedient German-Swiss to settle his own western lands, in the hope of displacing the disobedient and "barbaric" Scots-Irish with immigrants more apt to *be* impressed by his splendor. The myths and symbols of control were very much his stock in trade.[12]

Likewise Jefferson, albeit still more subtly and in a new age, dealt in similar items. His *Notes on Virginia* reveal an acute sensitivity to the charge that the new world and its inhabitants are inferior to things European, a claim he reverses at every opportunity.[13] Like Byrd's, his life and writings imply that a learned and yet accommodating, indeed in his case explicitly democratic, Virginia gentry was not only more enlightened than any European gentry but would maintain its leadership even in the face of the democratic sentiments aroused by revolution. He was right, but, again like Byrd, he was never sure that he was right. So, in building at Monticello his temple of himself as democratic aristocrat, he had built a house that was *also* an intimidating three-story Palladian pile high atop a dominating mountain. He, too, wanted it both ways, to be accommodating to, and to intimidate, his fellow whites. Building and rebuilding Monticello so that it finally achieved both aims bankrupted him.[14] As a result, he could not free his slaves; but this was no irony as, on this crucial point of slavery, he had raised Byrd's evasive ambivalence to an art form. Yes, slavery was unenlightened, but since slaves could not yet be freed, it was well they had enlightened masters.[15] This self-flattering ambivalence was built into the hegemonic myth itself. In sum, Jefferson, too, was obsessed with the myth of his class, with its status vis-a-vis European and local skeptics, and with using both suppleness and intimidation as means to control the delicate political environment of Virginia.

Let me not disguise the stunning success of these men and of their class. As Richard Beeman has pointed out, they alone of all the colonial elites south of Pennsylvania kept a reasonable control over the populace of their state during and after the revolution.[16] They did so because they got the blend of accommodation and intimidation just right. They thereby deserved that leadership of the country as a whole which they duly assumed in 1790 and maintained nearly intact until 1824. In the end time, and the ultimate hypocrisy of slavery, consumed them, but by then they had been masters of Virginia for well over a century and of the nation for almost a third of a century. But my point is not their success; my point is to suggest that the Virginia gentry maintained their power by ceaseless attention to their control and to their image, by ceaseless attention to the success and exact tone of their hegemonic discourse in all its forms. This is clearly true of Byrd and of Jefferson. It is also true of others. When they stumbled, as when an extravagant, debt-ridden gentry "borrowed" the public treasury in the 1760's in order not to lose their gloss of aristocracy, or as when troglodyte gentry tried simply to suppress the Baptist challenge to their authority in the same years, there was always an Edmund Pendleton to clean up the mess in the public finances before it became public, always a James Madison to persuade the planters that horsewhipping Baptists was out of style in an enlightened age. The myth was repaired and hegemony moved forward, ready for a new age. But it was all done by dint of constant awareness. Constantly challenged from above and from beneath, theirs was indeed a thin hegemony, stretched by many challenges, at once brittle and supple.

That the two most conscious mythmakers of this fragile class should have written the only two Anglo-American commonplace books I have seen so far that assemble a nightmare vision of women as the chaotic other of patriarchal power strikes me as quite possibly not an accident. Both men were also intensely concerned with maintaining authority within their families throughout their lives and this, too, may not be accidental.[17] What I am suggesting is that these two men were among the most concerned in a class remarkably concerned with mastery, and with building a successful image of gentility, concerned with a depth, breadth, and intensity unusual in the eighteenth-century world. So many things made their class potentially inferior; its distant provincial situation, its involvement in trade, its relatively free white constituency, and its slaveholding. Moreover, the domestic version of the many crises the Virginia gentry faced, in ultimately succeeding, was the struggle to muster resources adequate to a sufficient display and to their crafted self-image in an economy whose staple, tobacco, was first an unreliable boom-and-bust source of wealth, and then simply died in a long, slow whimper. Not only Byrds and Jeffersons, but increasingly men of other families, most notably the Lees, were raised to fury that they had to court women in order to obtain wealth, while watching family wealth of the previous generation pass not only to them but to their mothers, the widows, and to their sisters.[18] In Virginia perhaps more than elsewhere, wars for patriarchal resources became gender wars. The Virginia gentry had much to compensate for. Led by such mythmakers as William Byrd and Thomas Jefferson, they attempted to assuage their own feelings of inferiority, and to assuage the collective vulnerabilities of their class, by adjusting its mythology of mastery so that it at once perfected and surpassed the image of gentility borrowed from the metropolitan culture.

The Virginia gentry labored constantly at their control of their slaves, a control so total that it became to them the necessary definitional antithesis of their passionate conception of their own freedom. Perversely, their "benevolent" exercise of this power became in their own minds proof of their creativity, of a greater mastery. They labored as well, I am suggesting, or certainly their chief mythmakers, William Byrd and Thomas Jefferson did, at a complete and unruffled image of effortless domestic patriarchy, a power that Jefferson's generation thinly disguised as paternalism. The suppleness in their otherwise brittle conception of their own power lay, it seems to me, chiefly in their relations with lesser white males in the political arena. Indeed it is here that both Byrd and Jefferson sought to define lesser white males as something more than "the other," as forces that must *be* accommodated. Only for other white males, then, was their mastery truly found in their suppleness, and even there both Byrd and Jefferson made constant if in the latter case subtle recourse to the architecture of intimidation.[19]

For slaves, then, and certainly, to judge from today's evidence, for women as well, gentry hegemony as exercised by these two creators of the gentry's mythic world was a fragile and threatened control sustained by its totality more than by its suppleness. The mythic decision was to intimidate, not to accommodate. Where women were concerned this fact was literally discovered by these two men, in their commonplace books in the midst of their own ongoing acts of self-creation. Where constituents could not vote, theirs was a willful hegemony that brooked no opposition in its search for perfection amidst its own obvious imperfections. Slavery had perhaps already provided them with a model for such control, and it is possibly the willful rage of the slaveowner that we see in the hands of these fierce mythologizers, being applied to their parallel needs for control in the sphere of domestic patriarchy. In both cases, with slaves and with women, the struggle was to control persons who either constituted (slaves) or might seize control (women) of the resources that these patriarchs needed to realize their dream of themselves. Women who resisted, who did not fit into their picture of themselves, evoked a nightmare image of utter failure, utter chaos, in the minds of these passionately would-be gentlemen. It may be no accident, therefore, that just as Bali, that most theatrical of societies, gave rise to the works of Clifford Geertz, its dramaturgical anthropologist, so the Virginia gentry, the most staged and theatrical of gentries, gave rise to the work of Rhys Isaac, the quintessentially dramaturgical historian. For it seems possible that the imperatives of male patriarchy rode not just on Byrd's and Jefferson's but on that entire gentry's shoulders like, they would have said, a Harpy, but it was a male Harpy, and on the other shoulder rode the fear of their own illegitimacy. Just as, through performance, they controlled, so by controlling, they performed.

If this theory is correct, there was much of self-colonization in the entire process. While they were white, the Virginia gentry of the eighteenth century may recall the Indian gentry of the nineteenth, whose need to mimic the master culture of the colonizing power, England, created countless pathologies in its members. One of these pathologies surely lay in the accompanying need also to surpass the metropolitan model by turning provincial vices into moral virtues. So, in both respects, it was with the Virginia gentry. Control of slaves must be an asset not a vice, must be total yet benevolent, in a kind of mastery superior to that found in England. Control of women and the household must live up to the fullest imperatives of patriarchal power yet must appear benevolent so that, though slaveowners, these masters would appear the most perfect of patriarchs, really only model paternalists. Control of the white population must occur through intimidating display, yet, in meeting new world circumstances, by being accommodating as well, this exercise of power must be made to appear as superior not inferior to its old world equivalent. Truly, men of such mastery became god-like first movers of their own domestic and of far larger social worlds. But if William Byrd and Thomas Jefferson are any indication, the pathology, when this plan was disrupted by women at least, was rage. Rage at their failure to master and to surpass the masteries of the mother country. It is hard to know whether to call this self-colonization or hyper-colonization.

The great theoretician of the pathologies of colonial mimesis, Homi Bhabha, speaks of the inherent inappropriateness of the signifiers of colonial discourse, when applied in this manner. He notes that the continual need to mimic and to surpass inevitably creates something different, something which, in the eyes of the originals in England, is contemptible. It is, he says, "the difference between being English and being Anglicized." In this difference, "the ambivalence of colonial authority repeatedly turns from *mimicry*—a difference that is almost nothing but not quite—to *menace*—a difference that is almost total but not quite." The mimetic subjects are aware that in the end they cannot both mimic and improve on the model and are aware that in both these contradictory attempts small discrepancies from the master model arise, cumulatively creating an utter failure to be legitimate in terms of the original model. They are aware this thus excites contempt in England. It becomes evident to them that "history turns to farce and the presence [of the original] to a [mere] part [of the new-constructed colonial gentility]." This produces in them a "narcissism and paranoia that repeat furiously, uncontrollably."[20] I add that the narcissistic rage and paranoia produced by this inevitable failure are seated in a fear of the loss of identity and social chaos which would result from the inevitable failure of the mimetic effort. It is quite possibly this narcissistic rage that is being directed at women, here in Virginia, and this chaos which is being displaced onto them.

Whether this hypothesis can be broadened to include the construction of women by any vulnerable, marginal, or peripheral would-be patriarchs whose mimetic effort is unusually intense, and is marked by an effort simultaneously to mimic and to improve on a master model of authority—whether, in sum, it describes a pathology in the behavior of would-be gentlemen outside of Virginia and India—only time will tell.[21] Perhaps, even within the mother country, such self-colonization was the true gist of "Renaissance Self-Fashioning." To craft the self this intensely always implied, for the peripheral cases, failure and rage. The more broadly this behavior proves to be descriptive of eighteenth-century male behavior, the more we shall have to say that patriarchal rage was rage aimed by the failed patriarch at himself, and displaced onto women not so much as women but as obstacles to a mimesis that was doomed to failure or that, if successful, was liable to be brittle and self-conscious. Further, the more widely this syndrome is found, the more we shall have to say that a cosmology of power, nay of existence, in which women were identified with entropy, death, and dissolution was already characteristic of western culture before the age of the democratic revolutions. The necessity that these revolutions then posed, of progressively confining women's new-minted citizenship strictly to the domestic sphere, possibly came to be grounded on this nightmare cosmology, already evoked in the minds of brittle would-be patriarchs unable, in the face of the real powers of women, to carry their dreams of control into execution.[22]

Yet even if, within Virginia and perhaps elsewhere, this was the male nightmare behind the gendered nightmare we have seen, we must remember that a class's mythmakers in their worst moments do not necessarily represent their class even as myth or as hegemonic discourse. At most, this theory would explain the special pressures on William Byrd and Thomas Jefferson, explain why they so willfully invoked the terrible vision of gendered chaos they did invoke in their moments of defeat by women. It does not mean that such was the ideology of gender or the daily discourse of power in Virginia gentry households let alone in eighteenth-century country gentlemen's households in general. The true dimensions of patriarchy in Virginia and elsewhere have yet to be explored.

My guess would be that the whole process suggested here works something like this: the bits and pieces of the gendered nightmare here assembled are created in the dominant English culture by literary figures such as Milton, Otway, Rowe, and Young, and not always in utterly misogynistic contexts. These pieces are combined with older references dating at least back to the *Malleus Maleficarum* and are then assembled in actual usage by figures in England *and* by such as our two Virginia mythmakers. In Virginia our men are operating out of their special view of their own needs and of the needs of their class. These include the need to realize their own individual power within a larger and semi-mythic context, and the need, which both reveal in other writings, to mythologize the power of their provincial class in the face of its multiple illegitimacies and challenges, many of which do not exist in England. Even in Virginia, such misogynistic assemblages are made at vulnerable moments, moments of defeat by women, and are kept private. So what should concern us is not the egregiously assembled nightmare of gendered chaos in these two commonplace books, but the evidence of its penumbral associates, namely a preference for meek, clean, and obedient women, or for no women at all, which Byrd and Jefferson show throughout their remaining lives, or for snide public remarks about women, preferences shared to some degree by their associates. It is this sort of penumbra that is the real darkness cast upon women everywhere in the eighteenth century and that in my view was probably very deeply shadowed in Virginia. If as Carol Karlsen suggests, early America may be the place where Puritans came to be more pure, and so came down harder on women, then it may also be the place where patriarchal masters felt they had to exercise every aspect of patriarchal power, and where their master thinkers could not brook the very real defeats they inevitably incurred at the hands of women. If Virginia never quite became patriarchy's heaven, at least it gives us a good, solid glimpse of patriarchy's hell.

In the narrowest sense what I am proposing for Virginia alone, leaving its penumbral effects for women there and for men and women elsewhere left unspoken for the moment, is that Byrd and Jefferson epitomize the eternal vulnerability of a new-world, would-be gentry. Faced with contempt from England and skepticism from below, always anxious, always reconstituting themselves, enraged at the danger they will not succeed, enraged at obstacles, most notably at women, and lacking the full statutory buttressing which patriarchy received in Europe, they assembled a nightmare, gendered cosmology in which women received men's self-rage and fear of chaos.

To move forward into the nineteenth century, it is interesting to observe the continuing marginality of southern "aristocrats" in general. They insisted that they were central to the new nation, but slavery and their waning political power made them more peripheral to the United States than ever the Virginians had been to England. Perhaps we see, in their feudal pretensions and infamous willfulness and rage, now directed toward their political rivals in the north, a new stage of self-colonization, and a new, public intensity to their rage. Certainly their women seem to have gained leverage over them to reduce the burden of childbearing only by appealing to an image of women as meek and fragile. In the end, however, such "aristocrats" were disdained even by some of the would-be ideologues of a newer South, such as the improving farmer Edmund Ruffin. Their existence may have served chiefly only to create, in the Southern Belle, the very image of all their dreams of women, and of their own worst nightmares.[23]

CHAPTER 5

EPILOGUE: ON THE CONTEXTS OF MISOGYNY, 1450–1850

FOR hundreds of years, in early modern society, men assembled and reassembled misogyny in general and patriarchal rage in particular in many contexts, public and private. Here, we have examined primarily only one such context, one of domestic patriarchal rage privately expressed. There were many other misogynistic occasions, varying widely in their nature. There was never a single ideology or culture of misogyny behind these occasions, yet, and especially once print culture arrived, there was the consistent availability, in the midst of literally millions of printed fragments of previous cultural moments, of a mini-encyclopedia's worth of misogynistic utterances reaching back to such sources as the *Malleus Maleficarum*. Educated men took these from memory or from reading and modified them in a kind of ongoing male folklore and male construction of gender and the world. While this folklore and these constructions had a certain consistency, as the resemblances between the *Malleus* and Byrd's casting of superstition upon women show, the profile and politics of each reassembly were also unique. It is from the politics of each reenactment that we can learn most about the actualities of gender in historical situations and about the evolution of its construction by men. It is not enough simply to say that men were misogynistic. We must see how misogyny arose, functioned, and was shaped in particular historical settings.[1]

I have suggested that on the highest and most general level

what seems to have prompted the particular misogynistic constructions we have witnessed here was an inherent conflict between the idealization of patriarchy, as it was created by the emerging modern state, and the practical limitations that custom, law, and the state then placed upon men's actual power within their families. Frustration, rage, and misogyny could result from such a conflict between the ideal of masculine power and the realities of everyday life and of the prevailing legal regime. Yet I have also suggested that this is too general an hypothesis, and that certain would-be patriarchs, above all the mythmakers of a class of peripheral would-be gentlemen with questionable credentials and so a strong need to mimic the ideal patriarchal model, would be most vulnerable to failure. I have suggested that in such men we should see the highest degree of frustration, and of misogynistic rage, and that these emotions would to varying but significant degrees be shared if not always fully articulated by their entire class.

A parallel suggestion has been offered by Hanna Pitkin in her essay *Fortune Is a Woman*.[2] Pitkin suggests that the coalescence of misogyny and the gendering of power in Machiavelli's republican politics arose in a context in which medieval unities and traditional family roles were dissolving, leaving men of his class reliant upon themselves for whatever meanings they could construct. What Machiavelli appears to have constructed in such a context was a world in which women and sexuality tended to seduce men from the need to use their masculinity to achieve autonomy and a new order. Fickle, subversive, and possessive females were juxtaposed to ordering masculinity, female sexuality to male sublimation, misogyny to machismo. Thus was a new masculine, intellectualized, republican gentry to be built on the ruins of the traditional order. Pitkin's Machiavelli is so reminiscent of Byrd and above all of Jefferson as to need no further comment, save to note that if Machiavelli is any indication, not only gentries-in-the-making but those being remade were particularly vulnerable to such misogynistic genderings of their passionately desired power. Beneath their misogyny, they were all terrified of their own "effeminacy" and failure.

Carroll Smith-Rosenberg similarly depicts the vulnerability of commercial middle-class men in the early nineteenth-century United States, as they tried to make themselves out as the inheritors of the republican gentry of the revolutionary era.[3] The qualities they sought to possess were those of independence, disinterest, and civic virtue, properties not ordinarily associated with grasping merchants. Unsure of their right to possess this essentially aristocratic construction of their role as a justification for their growing power, these middle-class men purified themselves in turn by transferring to women the very disqualifying vices that the old gentry had accused them of possessing: women, and not middle-class males, it seems, were potentially corruptible and seducible, and so incapable of independence or of personal or civic virtue. Here, too, then, a gentry-in-the-making resorted to misogynistic transfers of its own fears about itself, to women.

Susan Juster's study of the masculinization of power and the feminization of sin by the male leadership of the New England evangelical churches in the late eighteenth-century United States adds the corollary that male leaders in maturing institutions temporarily peripheral to the larger culture in which they were set—as the evangelicals were, briefly, from 1776 to 1800—were also prone to an intense gendering of power.[4] Here, the male leaders of these churches simultaneously construed both sin and women as characterized by congenital unreliability, dissimulation, slander, and dissolution, while reliability and power became exclusively masculine and men's sins came to be seen as mere temporary aberrations.

There were variations in the misogynistic formulations employed or implied by these various males in various positions of vulnerability and ambition. Machiavelli, Byrd, and Jefferson shared a powerful fear not only of female sexuality but of a sudden reversal of power in which women controlled resources and male order dissolved. All three men sublimated their fears, and their drive for power and for order, into profound, constant intellectualization of their hoped-for position. The leaders of the evangelical churches, on the other hand, were in the position of casting women as subversive of their redeemed order in order to *remove* women from a doctrinal equality and a voting power they already possessed. In this instance there was no emphasis on subversive sexuality and no deep intellectualization, but only a view of women as inherently, politically, unreliable and subversive; there was no emphasis on a feared reversal of power, but only a need to reverse a sharing of power with women which had arisen when these churches were formed. Carroll Smith-Rosenberg's middle-class inheritors of republican virtue were a gentry in the making, yet they were in fact successfully inheriting gentry power if not virtue in any event and so their misogyny, while sexual, literary, and intellectualized, was simply not as intense as with Machiavelli, Byrd, and Jefferson. As will be seen, however, not only the differing structural situations of the men involved but also the passage of time may have played a role in the progressive tempering of the misogynies seen in these cases. But in all cases, the ones seen here, Pitkin's, Smith-Rosenberg's, and Juster's, vulnerable male elites characterized by not-fully-realized power are the misogynists.

Yet misogyny occurs closer to the center of the dominant culture as well. Susan Gubar's "The Female Monster in Augustan Satire" reveals that William Byrd's precise formulations of monstrous female desire, and the female bodily corruptions described in "The Female Creed," became powerfully articulated themes in the immediately succeeding years in the hands of Swift, Pope, Gay, and Fielding. Swift and Pope, above all, made corporeally corrupt, seducing, avaricious, hyper-effeminate women the symbols for a corrupt, avaricious, effeminate age in England. Like Byrd, Swift and Pope felt themselves peripheral to the main trends of early eighteenth-century England. Byrd was a rejected colonial; they were rejected Tory intellectuals in an age of corrupted whiggery. But in our minds at least, Swift and Pope are less marginal than Byrd, or even than Machiavelli. Their writings virtually became canonical in their own time and so placed misogyny in the center of English culture. In this way the misogyny of a marginal elite became canonical. Deborah Laycock takes this trend to centrality a step further with an almost contemporary case in her "Dreams and Bubbles: The Sexual Politics of South Sea Investment."[5] Here, roughly between 1700 and 1730, it was a new, marginal, and unstable phenomenon, the stock market, with its masses of fluid credit and wild waves of investment, speculation, and financial collapse, that became threatening to men at the very center of British power. The collapse of the South Sea Bubble in particular ruined many such men. As if in reply, writers such as Mandeville and Defoe metaphorically feminized credit as a lustful whore who led men to their ruin, in writings of unprecedentedly intense public misogyny. In their view female desire, still female even when it possessed men as well, had turned from the unlimited need for sex to the lust for unlimited gain, with the inevitable annihilating consequences for men. The image was probably spurred by the actual involvement of notable women, among them Lady Mary Wortley Montague, in the boom preceding the collapse. Women had freely entered this new, therefore marginal area of human activity and it was now said to be their actual and metaphorical lust, possessing women and men alike, that had led to chaos. In such an instance where an actual female presence intruded upon such a marginal, ungendered area of unstable power as the early London stock market, it was the very center of masculine power that reacted with misogyny.

Louis Montrose takes the argument yet further, in suggesting that still earlier in England's history a female sovereign, Elizabeth, had so upset the implicitly male gendering of power that English men from obscure butchers to Shakespeare and his audience felt compelled to subvert the unsettling symbolism of the Virgin Queen even while nominally praising it.[6] Men simply *had* to reconstruct a world where sexual, marital, familial, and political dominance was remasculinized, something Shakespeare does in assiduous detail in *A Midsummer Night's Dream*. The misogyny in this enterprise was only implicit, but if Montrose is right, it was no creation of marginal elites, but rather stood at the center of masculine fantasies in Elizabethan England. In sum, not only marginal and anomalous elites, but also established ones faced with the feminization of marginal and central areas of public life, were prone to misogyny, and to a nervous masculinization of power.

Do we want to proceed from these studies to the reductionist conclusion that in the early modern era all men, in their efforts to possess and even in their secure possession of power, were always inherently threatened by women's potential power over their masculine constructions of power, and so were inherently misogynistic? Possibly, but at least in theory, I would argue, it is still important to see these various occasions of reactualized, intense misogyny and of the regendering of power as a series of discrete political events each in its own context. The themes of men caught in changing, vulnerable, marginal positions, or of men in central positions surprised by a sudden coalescence of female power in areas either new or traditional, may in fact explain the major recrudescences of misogyny and gendering in the history of this era. Moreover, there is a powerful theme of male and of female agency which runs through all these examples. Misogyny in these intense forms is not automatic or inevitable, but rather certain men in specific political contexts choose visibly to reconstruct it, while others, in other contexts, do not. Female agency is a still stronger theme, as powerful and threatening women recur, running from prospective brides, actual wives, and inheriting widows to evangelical women with the vote in their churches, stock-market-investing ladies of fashion, and the Virgin

Queen herself. The battle of the sexes was fought on uneven terms, but women made it perhaps more of a contest than we have realized.

Within the accumulating evidence of female agency, one is struck by the recurrent evidence that it was often real *economic* power in the hands of women that excited a not-always-successful misogyny in men. In the case of New England witchcraft, as seen by Carol Karlsen in *The Devil in the Shape of a Woman,*[7] inheriting women, chiefly widows, seem to have been at the very core of Puritan men's fears of social disorder. Hence it was disproportionately often these women who were "witches." Yet even here, the vast majority of inheriting women were not accused as witches and, as far as the court records show, were not in fact dispossessed of property that was theirs by law. Deborah Laycock's possessing women, the actual female investors in the newly emerged stock market in London, went on investing and possessing from that time on. The women possessed of the patriarchal resources that William Byrd and the juvenile Thomas Jefferson longed to seize, the prospective brides, the wives and widows they faced, remained secure from these men at least. These women, like their New England counterparts, were tried as virtual witches, but only in the pages of the two Virginia mythmakers' commonplace books. The undetectable penumbral effects of such outbursts of male misogyny were surely repressive for these as for all women, but it is also important to see women as successful if harassed possessors of financial as of other resources, sufficiently firm in their possession to excite male nightmares.

Misogyny in the raw and *public* form to which some of the men seen here resorted, with corrupt or exaggerated female bodies, with women cast as whores and as vortices of superstition and entropy into which all male desire, reproduction, possession, and order were drawn, has a subsequent history that is also worthy of consideration. For even the examples cited here, most notably Byrd's "Female Creed" on its surface level, the indirect attack on women by Susan Juster's evangelical leaders, and the relatively gentle misogynistic accusations by Carroll Smith-Rosenberg's middle-class men, encountered after the turn of the nineteenth century, suggest that overt public misogyny had undergone an attenuation in the course of the eighteenth century. Much of the emphasis on female anatomy and explicit sexuality found, for example, in Mandeville and Defoe, in Swift and in Pope, and beneath the surface in Byrd's "Creed," waned.[8] Eventually entropy, annihilation, and death appeared less often on the list of female threats, though disorder itself never did leave the agenda.

As noted previously, Byrd's "Female Creed" may hint at the mechanisms by which this change occurred. In certain respects, "The Female Creed" parallels Swift's worst attacks on female bodily corruption, which Swift is not using just as a metaphor for social corruption but in fact horrifies and repels him. In an added irony, he is also unloading what is really his own lust and corporeality—for the "I" who speaks in "The Female Creed" is both Byrd and "woman"—on women as a necessary prelude to masculinizing and possessing that realm of pure mind, the enlightenment, in an act remarkably similar to Jefferson's own treatment of women in later life. Yet in Byrd the incontinent, pissing, farting women are at times almost a subtheme, a quick way of getting to and at larger social corruptions. Byrd's overall emphasis where women are concerned is on the broader but far more disembodied misogynistic point that women are superstitious. In the context of Byrd's adoption of enlightenment language, he is simply looking back at his own credulous past and unloading it on women. This is potentially a powerful and deadly device, but as he accomplishes it he renders women not so much superstitious and threatening, which they are in the *Malleus Maleficarum*, as simply unfashionable. In the face of Byrd's fear and hatred of women, their bodies, and their desires, as shown in the pages of his commonplace, and in the face of related disgust for women (and for the "woman" in himself) found in the subtext of "The

Female Creed," only the very enlightenment he is thereby embracing accounts for his relatively gentler treatment of women by consigning them to the attic of fashion in the main text of the "Creed." The enlightenment seems to have forced him into this position. Female witches, sick sexual fears, women as another, irredeemable race do not consort well with the optimistic rationalism and the faith in human improvement. Thus, Byrd has to deanatomize and desexualize women in the main argument of "The Female Creed" because to continue with an explicit, public demonology of women is itself no longer fashionable. It betrays the very rationality Byrd, and fashionable men in general, are trying to possess.

A further implication of the enlightenment would take decades longer to emerge, namely that rationality was inherent in the human brain regardless of gender. At that point extreme misogyny would truly be driven underground, along with superstition, bodily torture, fascination with bodily corruption, and dark unreason. It is this sanitization, decorporalization, and rational tidying of all human nature implicit in the enlightenment against which the Marquis de Sade was reacting when he ironically entitled his collection of fantasies of lust, with overtones of rape and sadism not untouched by misogyny, *Philosophy in the Bedroom.*[9] His wild protests were in vain, as a belief in the potential inherent rationality of all human beings, increasingly including white women as well as white men, had already made considerable headway. The democratic revolutions of the late eighteenth century would take this process a step further by raising implicitly an issue that before had been considered ludicrous, namely whether women could also in any sense be considered as active political citizens in a republic.

The cumulative dilemma that these intellectual changes posed for the public expression of old-fashioned misogyny, in which women's physical, sexual, and mental incapacities were so extreme and threatening as to render them nearly or actually witches, was captured in a magical historical moment in Massachusetts in 1778 in the midst of the American Revolution. There, in framing their suggestions for a revolutionary constitution, the leading men of wealthy Essex County had to explain why in their view women did not have sufficient discretion to be voters. They found themselves virtually *unable* to adopt the ancient misogynistic argument based on inherent incapacity. Instead, they spoke of a lack of "acquired" discretion in women that arose largely circumstantially. Women lacked acquired discretion "not from a deficiency in their mental powers" but from—and here they did have brief recourse to inherent tendencies—"the natural tenderness and delicacy of their minds." Evidently a new cage is being built here to contain the female animal; no longer a lustful, chaotic witch, she is, rather, too tender and delicate. Yet *any* argument that inherent tendencies disqualify women from participation is out of place in an enlightened, revolutionary age, so the gentlemen of Essex County quickly move on to a cultural and circumstantial argument. Women do not "acquire" sufficient discretion because of "their retired mode of life, and various domestic duties." "These," they continue, "concurring, prevent that promiscuous intercourse with the world, which is necessary to qualify them for electors."[10] It seems that the enlightenment and the revolution have forced these men to abandon, in public at least, the most misogynistic of the "inherent incapacity" arguments for disqualifying women from political life. In a naked moment, reaching for a new paradigm of containment, they virtually admit that women are too inexperienced to be voters because men keep them in a kind of purdah!

Clearly in such a polite, reasonable, equalitarian age, classic early modern misogyny of the kind found in Machiavelli, implied in the subtexts of Byrd's "Female Creed" and freely offered in Swift, had to sink underground. What we see in William Byrd's and Thomas Jefferson's commonplace books may be the pressures created by the increasing public unacceptability of the inner misogynistic rages these mythmakers felt; they had no full outlet for their rages save the intensely private medium they chose. Simultaneously, new public arguments had to be constructed for politically disqualifying women in an age that increasingly seemed to qualify them for public life. Or, in a particularly clever tactic, modes of partial but confined participation for women had to be constructed. Foremost among these were the mythologies of the "republican wife" and the "republican mother," that kept women as political citizens nicely confined to the home, where they could never have "promiscuous intercourse with the world" or truly "acquire discretion." But, as Jan Lewis has recently pointed out, women never served the republic well in this confined role. They functioned chiefly as symbols for affective values and for social solidarity that were being abandoned by a masculinized liberalism.[11] Confining women to the home and making them symbols for discarded social values was the subtle and perverse misogyny of the new, democratic age. Like the Southern Belle, the republican wife and mother were traps for women still seeking liberation.[12]

Beneath the surface of public life, however, another series of events appears to have unravelled itself in a more benevolent fashion with time. If the evidence offered here is any indication, for some time the domestic frustrations of patriarchs in general and of Virginia patriarchs in particular—frustrations born of the contrast between their theoretical and desired power and actual female control of resources and of some authority within the household—continued to play themselves out in daily life in spite of the apparent waning of harsh "patriarchy" into benevolent "paternalism." This frustration served as an ongoing source of intense private misogyny in the men most acutely aware of its implications for their hunger for genteel status. As it had been with William Byrd so it continued to be with Thomas Jefferson. Thus as public misogyny turned polite, private patriarchal misogyny still throve, for a time, and it probably played a role in limiting the spheres of the "republican wife" and "republican mother" at their very inception. But by the middle of the nineteenth century, in the United States at least, dowries and inheritances no longer determined a gentleman's success as much as before. In any event genteel status was drowned out by the rising power of a commercial-industrial elite with looser, indigenous models of gentility and with sufficient sources of wealth to achieve them. In such a middle-class context patriarchal rage made little sense and the sentimentalized family finally prevailed. Perhaps for this reason raw, private, patriarchal misogyny became nearly an empty province. Misogyny remained alive and well chiefly in what might be called its psychic roots, which had always been there and would be both explored and evinced by Sigmund Freud, and in its attenuated but still stifling public forms.[13]

NOTES

1. Commonplaces I: William Byrd

1. The standard work on commonplaces and on commonplace books is Joan Marie Lechner, *Renaissance Concepts of the Commonplaces* (N.Y., 1962): Erasmus's advice on how to keep a commonplace is in Desiderius Erasmus of Rotterdam, *On Copia of Words and Ideas* (*De Utraque Verborum ac Rerum Copia*; short reference *de Copia*), trans. and ed. Donald B. King and H. David Rix (Milwaukee, 1963); one of his collections of *topoi* is in English as *The Apophthegmes of Erasmus*, tr. Nicolas Udall (London, 1564), modern edition ed. Robert Roberts (Boston, England, 1877). The variations on the Erasmian theme, many arising from school practices, Puritan influences, personal whim and, eventually, a Lockean, enlightened emphasis on literal and codified knowledge of the world and of important arguments concerning it, soon blended with and nearly overwhelmed the pure Erasmian model as described in *de Copia* (King-Rix edition, p. 68 *et seq.*) and to some degree replaced its rhetorical transformations of *topoi* with more literal and accurate renderings or precise paraphrases. On the potential gendering of the genre itself, an issue not taken up here, see Felicity A. Nussbaum, *The Autobiographical Subject: Gender and Ideology in Eighteenth-Century England* (Baltimore, 1989), esp. 223–24.

2. The theory of language implied here is one implied in Roland Barthes, *Mythologies* (N. Y., 1972). For background see Lev Vygotsky, *Thought and Language* (Cambridge, Mass., 1989) and M. M. Bakhtin, *Speech Genres and Other Late Essays* (Austin, 1986); I am grateful to the linguist A. Becker of the University of Michigan for assistance with these theories, and thank as well Todd Gernes, a graduate student in American Culture at Brown University. Gernes's dissertation prospectus, "Political Expression and the Aesthetics of Affiliation: Young Women's Literary Culture in Nineteenth-Century America," applies many of these linguistic insights to the nineteenth century and at a time when commonplace books were becoming the province of women as much as of men.

3. One hardly need cite Clifford Geertz's many essays in this field, beginning with *The Interpretation of Cultures* (N.Y., 1973), or Marshall Sahlin's *Islands of History* (Chicago, 1985); but my own favorite example of the way cultural tropes

assemble and are enacted on specific occasions—with potentially disastrous results when two cultures strange to one another happen to be meeting—is Greg Dening's *History's Anthropology: The Death of William Gooch* (N.Y., 1988).

4. Stephen Greenblatt, *Renaissance Self-Fashioning: From More to Shakespeare* (Chicago, 1980).

5. Erasmus, *On Copia* (King-Rix edition, see esp. p. 68). John Locke, *A New Method of Making Common-Place Books* (Greenwood, London, 1706). Some of the commonplace books read for this paper are listed in chapter 4, note 10, below.

6. Michel Foucault, *The History of Sexuality: Vol. 1: An Introduction* (N.Y., 1978). "Feminist theory," or, more properly, "feminist scholarship" in general is so broad and varied a field that I need to be more specific here. In one sense, I refer to feminist writings on the origins and theory of patriarchy. The most familiar of these is Gerda Lerner's *The Creation of Patriarchy* (N.Y., 1986), but I have also found very useful Joan Kelly, *Women, History, and Theory* (Chicago, 1984), especially chapter 5, "Family and Society," 110–52. More specific studies of the praxis of patriarchal families in the seventeenth and eighteenth centuries are just beginning to emerge from feminist discourse, so here I have had to use pre-feminist scholarship, most notably Lawrence Stone's monumental *The Family, Sex, and Marriage in England* (London, 1977), and its American application as found in Daniel Blake Smith, *Inside the Great House: Planter Family Life in Eighteenth-Century Chesapeake Society* (Ithaca, 1980). But I have found that these latter works offer less help than expected on the contradictions of patriarchy in actual practice; for example, in Smith's book William Byrd comes across as by and large a successful patriarch! Rather, what I discover in my sources about patriarchy in practice seems to find echoes in feminist scholarship in other periods of American history. The hatred excited by women with real, and with financial power is reminiscent of the conclusions of Carol Karlsen, in *The Devil in the Shape of a Woman* (N.Y., 1987); the tendency of men to project their fears about their own loss of status onto women is echoed in an article by Carroll Smith-Rosenberg, "Domesticating Virtue: Coquettes and Revolutionaries in Young America," in *Literature and the Body: Essays on Populations and Persons* (Baltimore, 1989), 160–84. Finally, the depth to which male hatred and fear of women can go, the intensity of their pejorative gendering of the universe, recalls Susan Gubar's "The Female Monster," *Signs*, v. 3 n. 2 (Winter 1977), 380–94. These and other relevant works will be discussed and referenced later on appropriate occasions.

7. Byrd is treated in an essay by Kenneth A. Lockridge, *The Diary, and Life, of William Byrd II, 1675–1744* (Chapel Hill, 1987). His commonplace book is in the Virginia Historical Society, Richmond, Virginia, and with their permission is now being edited by Jan Gilliam, of the Collections staff at Colonial Williamsburg, whom I thank for the transcript used here, and by myself, for eventual publication in 1993. The earlier parts of the commonplace are treated in chapter 8 of "One of the Patriarchs: A Life of William Byrd II," a biography as yet

only partially complete. Erasmus's advice in *de Copia* (see note 1; King-Rix edition, p. 68) is a nearly perfect description of William Byrd's commonplace and Byrd's, in turn, is the purest example of an Erasmian commonplace among the fifty-odd studied to date. Its very purity in this schoolboy genre may testify yet again to the need of colonials to mimic perfectly and without variation the models taught them by and in the metropolis. The relevance of such a mimetic impulse is taken up in the conclusion to this essay. Because his entries often paraphrase, and virtually never identify his sources, it is very difficult to identify these but, as will be seen below (chapter 3, note 6), they seem to be largely classical or continental. The medical literature he seems to be drawing upon is consistent with that identified in Pierre Darmon, *Le mythe de la procréation à l'âge baroque* (Paris, Éditions du Seuil, 1981), but is selected or twisted to be more misogynistic.

8. This and all subsequent entries from the commonplace are taken or in a few cases paraphrased consecutively from the manuscript in and with permission of the Virginia Historical Society, 72–74, 78–84 in their pagination.

9. See Thomas Laqueur, *Making Sex: Body and Gender from the Greeks to Freud* (Cambridge, Mass., 1990), 99–103; as Laqueur points out, William Harvey had begun to drift away from this assumption in the seventeenth century, albeit evidently without refuting it, but it was not until the late eighteenth century that female orgasm began definitively to be separated from successful generation (Laqueur, 146–48; 161–63).

10. The letters (with a few pages of these missing) and the reflection are in the Byrd commonplace, Virginia Historical Society, 85–92.

11. Much of what precedes and follows is recounted in a preliminary essay on Byrd by Kenneth A. Lockridge, *The Diary, and Life, of William Byrd II.* The link to Filmer is documented in "Forum: *Albion's Seed* . . . A Symposium," *William and Mary Quarterly*, XLVIII, n. 2 (April 1991), 306–7.

12. The problems with Mrs. Dunn became manifest at the very end of Byrd's first diary, *The Secret Diary of William Byrd of Westover, 1709–1712*, ed. Louis B. Wright and Marion Tinling (Richmond, 1941), which ends in September of 1713, shortly before Byrd requested leave to go to England.

13. The "Dunella" letter is found in *The Correspondences of the Three William Byrds of Westover, Virginia, 1684–1776*, ed. Marion Tinling (Charlottesville, 1977), vol. 1, 275–80, and the uncertain date of Byrd's arrival in London is treated on p. 288, with the only certain evidence on 290. Even if in fact the "breeding" reference is to an unknown earlier pregnancy which ended in miscarriage, the facts remain that the earliest problems with Lucy and Mrs. Dunn immediately preceded Byrd's application for permission to go to England, and the "Dunella" letter, complaining about a long history of difficulties with his wife and Mrs. Dunn, must by the very length of these troubles date from some time after the initial hostilities between Byrd and Dunn, as captured in his diary for mid-1713, and therefore probably dates from sometime in 1714, or within a year of his

actual departure for London. This puts Byrd's problems with his household in far closer proximity to his decision to leave (late 1713) and to his actual departure (early-to-mid-1715) than the political and financial problems, which arose as early as 1711 and 1712, and which were the nominal reasons for his excursion to England. Since the "Dunella" letter itself strongly implies sexual estrangement and virtually threatens separation or even divorce, we are entitled to ask whether Byrd's departure from Virginia was not in the end precipitated by a need to escape from insoluble problems within his marriage and household.

14. Again, all this is documented in Lockridge, *Diary, and Life, of William Byrd II.*

15. Michel Foucault, *The History of Sexuality: Vol. I.* See especially part 3: "Scientia Sexualis," 53–73.

16. Thomas Laqueur, *Making Sex,* esp. 25–154.

17. For example, see Laqueur, *Making Sex,* 144; Laqueur amplified this possibility in conversations and seminars while visiting fellow at the Institute for the Humanities, University of Michigan, in October-November 1990.

18. Laqueur, *Making Sex,* 148–243.

2. *"The Female Creed": Misogyny Enlightened?*

1. "The Female Creed" is in *Another Secret Diary of William Byrd of Westover,* ed. Maude H. Woodfin and Marion Tinling (Richmond, 1942), 449–75. Gubar's "The Female Monster" (see note 6, chapter 1, above) and Deborah Laycock's "Dreams and Bubbles: The Sexual Politics of South Sea Investment," delivered at the Western Meeting of the Society for Eighteenth-Century Studies, San Diego, February 1991 (Professor Laycock is in the Department of English, University of Iowa), leave little doubt that, until the mid-eighteenth century, there were virtually no limits on publicly printed misogyny in England, and suggest that if anything the intensity of public misogynistic discourse peaked between 1690 and 1740.

2. Misogyny remained active in the printed medical literature, however, and under this "scientific" disguise probably became more marked with time: see Thomas Laqueur, *Making Sex* (note 9, chapter 1, above).

3. Keith Thomas, *Religion and the Decline of Magic* (N.Y., 1971).

4. For more male misogyny prompted by the South Sea Bubble, see Deborah Laycock, "Dreams and Bubbles," referred to in note 1, above.

5. Gubar, "The Female Monster," 388–89.

6. *Malleus Maleficarum,* Henry Kramer and James Sprenger, trans., ed. and with an introduction by Montague Summers (London, 1928).

7. The quotation "one of the patriarchs" is in Byrd, *Correspondence* (see note 13, chapter 1, above), v. I, 355, letter to Charles Boyle, Earl of Orrey, July 5, 1726; the critique of slavery is in *Correspondence,* II, 487, in a letter to Lord Egmont.

8. This feminization of superstition has been noticed in passing in Peter

Wagner's paper on another aspect of "The Female Creed," "The Female Creed: William Byrd as Ribald Satirist," unpublished paper, Peter Wagner, Department of Modern Languages, University of Aston in Birmingham, and Jan Lewis's current research includes an inquiry into a similar phenomenon in Hamilton's *Federalist* essays.

9. This is the so-called Stretch catalog, made in 1777 before the library was sold, and printed in John Spenser Bassett, *The Writings of Colonel William Byrd of Westover in Virginia, Esquire* (N.Y., 1901), 413–43.

10. Keith Thomas, *Religion and the Decline of Magic*, footnotes all of these authors under his discussions covering the same beliefs Byrd chronicles in "The Female Creed."

11. Henry Bourne, *Antiquitates Vulgares, or, The Antiquities of the Commonplace People* (Newcastle, 1725). I am grateful to my colleague Thomas Tentler for this reference.

12. Bourne, *Antiquitates*, Preface.

13. Bourne, *op. cit., loc. cit.*

14. See Kenneth Lockridge, *The Diary, and Life, of William Byrd II* (note 7, chapter 1, above), 43–5.

15. See *Another Secret Diary*, January-February 1718.

3. Commonplaces II: Thomas Jefferson

1. *Jefferson's Literary Commonplace Book*, ed. Douglas L. Wilson, in Papers of Thomas Jefferson, Second Series (Princeton, 1989).

2. Locke's advice was in a letter to a French friend, published posthumously as *A New Method of Making Common-Place-Books* (see note 5, chapter 1, above).

3. For the history of this notion of "literature," see "How 'Poesy' Became 'Literature': Making and Reading the English Canon in the Eighteenth Century," unpublished paper by Trevor Ross, Erindale College, University of Toronto, 1990. One wonders, however, whether it was not mere "poesy" instead of true "literature," in Ross's terms, which Jefferson saw himself as including in his commonplace, as the young Jefferson clearly lacked the critical distancing required for the newly conceived perusal of "literature." To the contrary, his chief standard seems to be the personal appropriation of rage, rebellion, and misogyny wherever they could be found, a mode of use of canonical texts which Ross identifies as potentially archaic by Jefferson's time (p. 8, etc.). For Jefferson, the canon was mere "poesy," reflective of contemporary ideological values, and not "literature" to be distanced and critiqued.

4. See Douglas Wilson's critical introduction and appendices to *Jefferson's Literary Commonplace Book*. Careful use of his dating, and of his portrait of the implicit original behind Jefferson's reorganization of the book in 1768, has permitted the partial reconstruction of the original of 1762–1764 as offered here. The number Wilson assigns to each entry, based on its placing in 1768, is cited in this text, and a look at Wilson's critical apparatus will permit the

reader to judge the accuracy of his, and my, reconstruction of the surviving original sequences. In any event as the text, below, makes clear, large sections of these sequences—nearly all those used here—were left intact by Jefferson in 1768, so any "reconstruction" serves mainly to delete later material inserted in or between these sequences in 1768. The chief gap is that material originally found *between* the sequences cited from the *earlier* Jefferson commonplace, and dropped in his reorganization of 1768, cannot be recovered.

5. Wilson, *Jefferson's Literary Commonplace Book*, p. 213 notes that this sequence, dominated yet again by themes of power and misogyny, was entered slightly later in the pre-1763 period, and gives Wilson's grounds for this evaluation.

6. Byrd obscures his sources, but in several cases it is clear that he is not only selecting for misogyny from out of the vast range of anecdotes available, but is selecting or creating more misogynistic anecdotes than the standard version of the tales he uses. For example, earlier in the commonplace (p. 18) he relates Diogenes' tale of "Astrologers . . . [who] peep into the stray motions of the Planets above [yet] know nothing of the stray motions of their wives below." Yet in Erasmus's *Apophthegmes* (see note 1, chapter 1, above) the same tale, while equally bemused by the fuzzy-headedness of astrologers, makes no mention of stray wives at all. Since Erasmus was so obviously the pattern for Byrd's commonplace, and since Byrd had Erasmus's collection of classical anecdotes in his library (see Stretch catalogue referred to in note 9, chapter 2, above), the indication is that Byrd either selected a more misogynistic version of the tale from another source, or—following Erasmus's advice to put tales into his own rhetoric—crafted his own, more misogynistic version.

Another example, this one from Byrd's misogynistic passages, makes the same point. The story about "Popilia . . . being asked . . . why [female] Brutes would never admit the male after they had once conceived," and answering "because they are Brutes, and know no better" is found in Konrad Lycosthene's standard, *Apophthegmata* (London, 1596), and is there attributed to Macrobious's *Saturnalia*. But the version Byrd uses or which, in accordance with Erasmus's advice to rework apothegms in one's own langauge, he creates, adds that Popilia answered "with the true Spirit of a woman," thereby underlining the point that unrestrained lust is typical of woman.

Similarly, two of Byrd's tales of powerful female desire, including the one about the insatiable Messalina, orginally found in Juvenal, are also found in Brantôme, *Vies des dames galantes* (originally sixteenth century, English edition is trans. A. R. Allinson, intro. G. Harsdörfer, *Lives of Fair and Gallant Ladies* [Citadel-Liveright, N.Y., 1933], 20, 364–66. Whether or not Byrd took these anecdotes from Brantôme, the French author's work demonstrates how the exact same tales *can* be placed in a gentler context, in which both male and female desires range from gallantry to occasional excess. Brantôme's charming courtly contexting of these stories contrasts sharply with Byrd's merciless use of them in his single-minded depiction of threatening female sexuality. Thus, whether or not Byrd took his two quotes out of this context, as he may have, or twisted their wording toward misogyny, as he seems not to have done, he certainly seems to be creating a context in which each tale acquires an ominous point, which as Brantôme demonstrates, it need not have.

But with Jefferson, the de-contexting and relentlessly misogynistic re-contexting of quotations is far more marked. That Jefferson could have constructed a more favorable version of woman using Milton, for example, and that others did precisely this, can be seen in Jan Lewis's "The Republican Wife: Virtue and Seduction in the Early Republic," *William and Mary Quarterly*, XLIV, n. 4 (October 1987), 703–7. The misogynistic speeches from Otway and Rowe are simply ripped from a contrary context in each case; Otway's *Orphan* is used here as edited by Aline M. Taylor (Lincoln, 1976) and Rowe's *Fair Penitent* as edited by Sophie C. Hart (Boston, 1907). For critical commentaries on *The Orphan* see Taylor's introduction to the play and Derek Hughes, "The Orphan: An Interpretation," *Durham University Journal*, new series v. 44, n. 2 (1983), 45–54; Gail E. Aagaard, "A Critical Study of the Plays of Thomas Otway," Dissertation Abstracts International, v. 41 (April, 1981), 4401A. Both Otway and Rowe are treated in Veeka Tumir, "She Tragedy and Its Men: Conflict and Form in *The Orphan* and *The Fair Penitent*," *Studies in English Literature*, v. 30, nr. 3 (Summer 1990), 411–28. Rowe alone is treated in J. H. Armisted, "Calista and the 'Equal Empire' of Her 'Sacred Sex,' " *Studies in Eighteenth-Century Culture*, v. 15 (1986), 170–85. See also Katherine H. Rogers, "Masculine and Feminine Values in Restoration Drama: The Distinctive Power of Venice Preserved," *Texas Studies in Literature and Language*, v. 27, n. 4 (Winter 1985), 390–404, and Richard Dammers, "Female Characterization in English Platonic Drama: A Background for the Eighteenth-Century Tragedies of Nicholas Rowe," *Restoration and Eighteenth-Century Theatre Research*, v. 1, n. 2 (Winter 1986), 34–41.

7. Again, Wilson, *Jefferson's Literary Commonplace Book* gives citations and often suggests specific editions for the works cited by Jefferson.

8. Jack McLaughlin, *Jefferson and Monticello: The Biography of a Builder* (N.Y., 1988), 47–51. Fawn Brodie first developed the idea of Jefferson's conflict with his mother, in *Thomas Jefferson: An Intimate History* (N.Y., 1974), but she did not have the edited and reconstructed commonplace book which McLaughlin uses.

9. *Op. cit., loc. cit.*

10. McLaughlin's portrait of Martha Wayles Jefferson is in *op. cit.*, 109, 157, 156, 168, 177–88, 192–207, 231, 341, 345, 450.

11. Jefferson's letter to Martha is of January 7, 1798, as cited in McLaughlin, *op. cit.*, 194. The connection between sexuality and cleanliness in Jefferson's mind was first taken up in Winthrop Jordan, *White over Black* (Chapel Hill, 1968), 461–68; the quotation from Jordan is on p. 462. In fact, Jordan brilliantly exposes Jefferson's entire peculiar sexual psychology in these pages, in a way perfectly consonant with my own and McLaughlin's analysis of the common-

place, using only the letters and other sources, and not the commonplace at all.

12. The possible influence of French models is touched upon but its significance is not fully developed in McLaughlin, *op. cit.*, 209–38. McLaughlin also plays with the idea that Monticello became also a "hermitage," a refuge from "the crush of too much family in too little space" as experienced in his youth; but while his book provides much of the description used in the following analysis he does not systematically treat Monticello as a house in which family, and women, are suppressed. In general, therefore, the analysis which follows is my own, and is based not only upon the material in McLaughlin's book but on two visits to Monticello and on conversations with Mark Wenger, on the architectural history staff of Colonial Williamsburg. Parts of this analysis were developed in an illustrated lecture delivered at the Museum of Early Southern Decorative Arts in Salem, North Carolina, and at Colonial Williamsburg, in July 1988, before I had read McLaughlin's superb book, and it appeared subsequently in another form in a review of McLaughlin's book in the *Pennsylvania Magazine*, CXV, n. 1 (January 1991), 120–23. Nonetheless, as the review notes, McLaughlin's informed and imaginative pioneering reconstruction of Jefferson's literal and figurative constructions of Monticello has enriched my views and leads us powerfully to this interpretation of the house. It should be noted, too, that by 1794, when Jefferson began conceiving the new Monticello, his daughter Patsy was married, and in subsequent years she and her children spent much time at Monticello, yet Jefferson nonetheless designed it as a house in which women and family were suppressed.

13. Letter of January 31, 1801, as cited in McLaughlin, *Jefferson and Monticello*, 269.

4. On the Sources of Patriarchal Rage

1. Again, the reference is to volume one of Foucault's *History of Sexuality* (see note 6, chapter 1, above), esp. 53–73.

2. Public misogynistic rage was, however, not unheard of, as is made startlingly clear in a recent paper by Deborah Laycock, "Dreams and Bubbles: The Sexual Politics of South Sea Investment" (see note 1, chapter 2, above). This and other references to the wider literature on misogyny will be taken up in chapter 5, below.

3. Byrd had earlier labelled another woman who rejected him a "bitch." See K. Lockridge, *The Diary, and Life, of William Byrd II* (see note 7, chapter 1, above), 93.

4. The references to Foucault and to feminist scholarship in this passage are essentially those cited in chapter 1, note 6, above.

5. Ann Kibbey, *The Interpretation of Material Shapes in Puritanism: A Study of Rhetoric, Prejudice, and Violence* (Cambridge, England, 1986).

6. As to whether there was an ongoing misogynistic male "ideology" in a

more general form, I must admit that there is a loose tradition or a recurrence of various misogynistic ideas, albeit in different forms in different contexts, which gives credence to this idea of a male "ideology." Thus, there was nothing *entirely* new or unique about Byrd's or Jefferson's views as seen here. The ideas that women were superstitious, found in Byrd's "The Female Creed," and that their desires for sex and power were uncontrollable and led to evil and chaos, so prominent in both Byrd's and Jefferson's commonplaces, can be found in the *Malleus Maleficarum*, written in the fifteenth century by two German monks. Chaotic female lust for possessions as well as for sex would enter into a complex portrait of what Susan Gubar (see note 6, chapter 1, above) has called "The Female Monster," found in the writings of Swift and Pope in the years immediately following Byrd's essay and entries. But not all men on all occasions invoked misogynistic images, nor did those men who did do so in the same context or with the same nuances or profile. There was always a specific politics to every occasion on which misogyny was re-enacted and recast. Hence each misogyny had its own profile; the *Malleus*, Swift and Pope, Byrd and Jefferson are not synonymous. Two monks obsessed about witchcraft, two Tory writers concerned about the corruptions of their age, and two Virginia gentlemen preoccupied with power over specific patriarchal resources do not suggest a uniform origin, etiology, profile, or significance for all of these occasions of misogyny. We must learn what we can from each case. What we are after now is the politics of the private misogyny here practiced by William Byrd and Thomas Jefferson; the wider politics of these and the multiple further occasions of misogyny found in the literature will be treated in chapter 5.

7. Lynn Hunt, in "Forum: Beyond Roles, beyond Spheres: Thinking about Gender in the Early Republic," *William and Mary Quarterly*, XLVI, n. 3 (July 1989), 579; paper by Joel Harrington, Department of History, Vanderbilt University, "Hausvater and Landesvater: The Patriarchal Alliance and its 'Restoration' of Marital Order in Sixteenth-Century Germany," delivered at the Annual Meeting of the American Historical Association, New York, December 29, 1990.

8. *The Works of George Savile, Marquess of Halifax*, ed. Walter Raleigh (Oxford, 1912), pp. 7–25: originally published as *Miscellanies by the Right Noble Lord, the Late Lord Marquess of Halifax, viz: I: Advice to a Daughter [etc.]* (London, 1700).

9. See Gordon Schochet, *Patriarchalism in Political Thought* (Blackwell, Oxford, 1975); Rhys Isaac, "Communication and Control: Family Government, Law, and the Feelings at Colonel Carter's Sabine Hall, Virginia, 1752–1778," in Sean Wilenz, ed., *Rites of Power* (Philadelphia, 1985); and Jay Fliegleman, *Prodigals and Pilgrims: The American Revolution against Patriarchal Authority* (N.Y., 1982).

10. Many of the other commonplace books consulted, and most particularly those in the Virginia Historical Society at Richmond, are scarcely commonplace books at all, but rather day books, account books, or books of notes reminders,

interesting in many ways but not for this comparison. Of the sources which bear greater resemblance than the foregoing to the genre as Byrd and Jefferson define it, some of those consulted are as follows:

At The Bodleian Library, Oxford University; English Commonplace Books: Richard Paul Jodrell, *Mucrones Verborum Dramatick Observations* (circa 1775–1776), Ms. English Msc C-271; Anon., 1687, no title, Ms. Engl. Msc. C. 34; Richard Frank, no title, circa 1729–1754, Ms. Engl. Msc. C-275; E. C. Wallis? *A Brief Summary of Logic; or, The Art of Reasoning*, Ms. Engl. Msc. F-420; Anon., no title, 1566–1603(?), Ms. Engl. Msc. D-28; Robert Trail, no title, 1755, Ms. Engl. Msc. F-79; others from Engl. Msc. Ms. consulted include Francis Blomefield?, a collection Martiniano, 1736 F-18; Thomas Fuller?, no title, mid-1600's? G-6; Anon., no title, 1777–79 E-46.

At the American Antiquarian Society, Worcester, Mass.; New England Commonplace Books: William Bentley Papers, v. 4, V.S. 16–24, Commonplace Books, 1780's-1820's; John Saffin, Notebook, 1665–1708, typescript of original in Rhode Island Historical Society; John Sparhawk, Notebook, 1660's?; Cotton Mather, *Quotidiana*, 1690's, and Samuel Mather, Collectiones Miscellanea, 1723, both in the Mather Family Papers; Nathan Fiske, Notebook, 1750–1795?; Thomas Collins, Notebook, 1759; William Sheldon, Notebooks, ca. 1789- ; Anon., Commonplace Book, circa 1771-, filed under "Quotations" by the AAS; Ebeneezer Parkman, Extracts, ca. 1712–1779, Parkman Family Papers, Box 2, Folder 5.

At the Huntington Library, San Marino, California; English Commonplace Books: Anon., no title, ca. 1792, HM34804; Anon., no title, circa 1635, HM 1338; Thomas Grocer, Daily Observations, 1657, HM93; Thomas Percy, no title, seventeenth century, HM216; John Denham, no title, seventeenth-eighteenth century, HM 30309; Anon., A collection of the best Poems, Lampoons, Songs, & Satires from the Revolution of 1688 to 1792, EL8770.

At the Huntington Library; Virginia Commonplaces: Robert Bolling, La Gazetta, or Poems, Imitations, Translations, 1764–1768?, BR73; Robert Bolling, A Collection of Diverting Anecdotes, Bons Mots, and other Trifling Pieces, 1764, BR164. *At the William L. Clements Library, Ann Arbor, Michigan; Virginia Commonplaces:* Landon Carter, entries in Virginia Almanack, 1766–1767; Robert Wormley Carter, entries in Virginia Almanack, 1764–1765.

At the Virginia Historical Society, Richmond; Virginia Commonplaces: see evaluation at beginning of this note.

Misogyny is rarely encountered at all in this tremendously varied and far from exhaustive list of the "commonplaces" consulted, a collection which otherwise serves chiefly to illustrate the incredible variety of this "genre" even once day books, account books, etc., are ruled out. Of all of those cited, Saffin's (AAS, above) is closest to William Byrd's as a period sub-genre, and Bolling's quasi-commonplaces (Huntington, above) are closest to Jefferson's. Neither Saffin nor Bolling is notably misogynistic and Bolling's "La Gazetta" and "Collection" taken together, both entirely from the 1760's, in fact demonstrate that a commonplace can handle the wars of the sexes in an even-handed fashion. On being rejected by a woman, he shows a fleeting misogyny balanced by love and by an awareness of male failings. Thus, there is no inevitable invocation of intense, imbalanced misogyny in what was at this point in time (1600–1800) largely a male genre. Only certain men, and, in this study so far, only two of the Virginia gentry's chief mythmakers, used the genre to assemble a powerfully extended misogynistic vision; and in both cases this occurred in the specific context of a failed struggle for control of or access to patriarchal resources in a domestic context. The purpose of this paper is to see what this constellation of events might signify.

11. The preceding and following descriptions of the evolution of the Virginia gentry are implicit in Edmund S. Morgan, *American Slavery, American Freedom: The Ordeal of Colonial Virginia* (N.Y., 1975), and in Rhys Isaac, *The Transformation of Virginia* (Chapel Hill, 1982); the main themes are more explicit in Kenneth A. Lockridge, *Settlement and Unsettlement in Early America: The Crisis of Political Legitimacy before the Revolution* (N.Y., 1981), and in Lockridge, *The Diary, and Life, of William Byrd II* (see note 7, chapter 1, above), where the quotations from Byrd are found.

12. Lockridge, *The Diary, and Life, of William Byrd II*, 122–66.

13. Thomas Jefferson, *Notes on Virginia*, ed. W. Peden (Chapel Hill, 1954); Jefferson's works in general can be found in an older edition, *The Writings of Thomas Jefferson*, ed. Albert E. Bergh (20 vols. Washington, D.C., 1907); but this has largely been supplanted by the continuing multi-volume modern edition, *The Papers of Thomas Jefferson*, first series ed. Julian Boyd, second series ed. Charles T. Cullen (Princeton, 1950–1989). The standard biography is Dumas Malone *Jefferson and His Time* Vol. 1, *Jefferson the Virginian* Vol. 2, *Jefferson and the Rights of Man* (Boston, 1948, 1951).

14. See previous text and Jack McLaughlin, *Jefferson and Monticello* (see note 8, chapter 3, above).

15. Jefferson's ambivalence on this subject reached a peak at the time of the Missouri Crisis, and was expressed in a letter to John Holmes, written on April 22, 1820; see *The Writings of Thomas Jefferson*, ed. Paul Leicester Ford (N.Y., 1899), vol. 10, 157–58.

16. Richard Beeman, "The Political Response to Social Conflict in the Southern Backcountry: A Comparative View of Virginia and the Carolinas during the Revolution," in *An Uncivil War: The Southern Backcountry during the American Revolution*, ed. Ronald Hoffman and Thad Tate (Charlottesville, 1985), 213–39.

17. My views on Jefferson within his family have been shaped by conversations with Bryn Roberts, a graduate student at the University of Michigan familiar with the record of Jefferson's personal life in the years after 1800. A look at the standard editions of Jefferson's letters (see notes 13, 14 in this chapter), especially where these include family letters to, from, and about Jefferson, will confirm this view.

18. The reference to the Lees, above, is from Paul Nagel, *The Lees of Virginia: Seven Generations of an American Family* (N.Y., 1990).

19. On Byrd and accommodation, see Lockridge, *The Diary, and Life, of William Byrd II* (see note 7, chapter 1, above); Jefferson's willingness to praise, and to cultivate the votes of the American yeoman farmer is too well known to need comment and was the essence of his "democratic" ideology. The most powerful commentary on the contrast between the treatment of slaves and the accommodation shown lesser white males is in Morgan, *American Slavery, American Freedom* (see note 11, this chapter). In some respects I am here simply adding white women to Morgan's list of the "others" who were the definitional opposites of gentry power and on whom intimidation could be practiced.

20. Homi Bhabha, "Of Mimicry and Men: The Ambivalence of Colonial Discourse," *October*, v. 34 (Fall 1985), 125–33. Lockridge, *The Diary, and Life, of William Byrd II* documents the mimetic urge in this especially intense and almost pathological case and in his son; Jefferson's urge was, even more than Byrd's, to mimic while reconstituting gentility in superior, accommodating, American terms, an urge implied in his *Notes on Virginia* and embodied, as noted, in Monticello itself. John Shy has documented the power of the mimetic urge in George Washington, and has extended the argument outside Virginia by including Benjamin Franklin in the near-pathology of this state; see John Shy, "Franklin, Washington, and a New Nation," *Proceedings of the American Philosophical Society*, vol. 131, n. 3 (1987), 308–24, esp. 315–22. Franklin, I might add, was also an intensely misogynistic man.

21. The argument here parallels that offered for the treatment of women by self-colonized *middle*-class men in the *nineteenth* century by Carroll Smith-Rosenberg in her "Domesticating Virtue: Coquettes and Revolutionaries in Young America" (see chapter 1, note 6, above). Essentially, the process of self-colonization with gentry ideals, mimetic culture, and the displacement onto women of rage and of the vices of failure as feared by men within themselves, seems simply to have moved down through the class structures as gentility was progressively Americanized, then democratized, over the eighteenth and nineteenth centuries. The difference between us is that I see the process as evoked by specific occasions of female power which threaten successful male mimesis, whereas Smith-Rosenberg seems to feel the process was inevitable and automatic, detached from specific gender confrontations over power and resources. On this point I tend to agree more with Carol Karlsen (*The Devil in the Shape of a Woman*; see note 6, chapter 1, above), with Deborah Laycock (see note 1, chapter 2, above), and with Susan Juster (see notes to chapter 5, below) that specific occasions of female power, primarily albeit not solely economic power, tend to provoke coalescences of male misogyny and the extreme gendering of power. It is not an automatic process, but one made up of an ongoing if sometimes highly local series of power confrontations. In this process, in my view, women are at a great disadvantage but they do not always lose, in the short run. Hence male rage.

22. But if so, the grounding in nightmare was by then well hidden. Both the enlightenment and the democratic revolutions later in the century made it difficult for men to indulge openly in misogynistic rages based in fears bordering on superstition and vehemently denying women any right to a political role. See the discussion in chapter 5, following.

23. The study of Virginia women's efforts to reduce the burden of child-bearing is Jan Lewis and Kenneth Lockridge, "Sally Has Been Sick: Virginia Gentry Women on Pregnancy and Childbirth, 1780–1830," *Journal of Social History* (Summer 1988), 5–19. The best essay on the Southern Belle is in Shirley Abbot, *Womenfolks: Growing Up Down South* (N.Y., 1983).

5. *Epilogue: On the Contexts of Misogyny*

1. In the same spirit, it is also true that *Malleus Maleficarum* would be simplified grossly by reading it only as a kind of ur-text for European and American misogynists, rather than as a text parts of which share, for complex reasons, a misogynistic folklore parts of which in turn are later found in more purely misogynistic contexts, as in, for example, Byrd's commonplace. The latter, at any rate, is the view implicit in Carlo Girzburg, *Ecstasies: Deciphering the Witches, Sabbath* (N.Y., 1991), who argues powerfully against reducing the European witchcraft tradition to simply misogyny, an argument which could be extended even to the *Malleus*.

2. Hanna Fenichel Pitkin, *Fortune Is a Women: Gender and Politics in the Thought of Niccolo Machiavelli* (Berkeley, 1984).

3. Carroll Smith-Rosenberg, "Domesticating Virtue" (see note 6, chapter 1, above), 160–184.

4. Susan Juster, Department of History, University of California Santa Barbara, "'Surely the Tongue Is an Unruly Member': Representations of Women in the Evangelical Community, 1740–1840," paper presented at the Western Meeting of the Society for Eighteenth-Century Studies, San Diego, California, February 9, 1991.

5. Professor Laycock is in the Department of English, University of Iowa, and the paper was delivered on the same occasion as the paper by Susan Juster, documented in the footnote above.

6. Louis Adrian Montrose, "'Shaping Fantasies': Figurations of Gender and Power in Elizabethan Culture," *Representations*, 1:2 (Spring 1983), 61–94.

7. Carol Karlsen, *The Devil in the Shape of a Woman* (see note 6, chapter 1, above).

8. For Mandeville and Defoe, see the paper by Deborah Laycock cited in the text and note 5. For evidence that misogyny did indeed grow milder as the eighteenth century wore on, see Felicity A. Nussbaum, *The Brink of All We Hate: English Satires on Women, 1660–1750* (Lexington, 1984), 160–61.

9. Donatien-Alphonse de Sade, *The Marquis de Sade: The Complete Justine, Philosophy in the Bedroom, and Other Writings* (N.Y., 1965). This analysis of de

Sade is parallel to that offered by Foucault in *The History of Sexuality Vol. 1*, An Introduction (Vintage edition, N.Y., 1980), 148–49.

10. Robert J. Taylor, ed., *Massachusetts, Colony to Commonwealth: Documents on the Formation of Its Constitution, 1775–1780* (Chapel Hill, 1961), 81.

11. Jan Lewis, "Motherhood and the Construction of the Male Citizen in the United States, 1750–1850," forthcoming in George Levine, ed., *Constructions of the Self* (New Brunswick, 1992). The process of masculinizing the American Revolution as described here has parallels with Joan Landes's account of a very similar process in the French Revolution, and in the latter case it is clear that, once again, it was real female power which prompted the masculine reaction; see Joan Landes, *Women and the Public Sphere in the Age of the French Revolution* (Ithaca, 1988).

12. The findings reported in this monograph are in many ways consistent with the work of Carole Pateman on the emergence of modern political contract theory in the seventeenth and eighteenth centuries (*The Sexual Contract*, Stanford, 1988). She observes that John Locke's social contract implicitly included an earlier "sexual contract" which provided for the subordination of women within the family. Thus, while the Lockean language of individual participation in a rational political contract seemed to free women equally with men, mothers, wives, and daughers as well as sons, from the bonds of classic patriarchal power, in fact it did not. Explicitly within the family and implicitly in civil society, women remained the subjects of male authority and less than full individuals. The continuing presence of patriarchal rages well into the eighteenth century, and the arrival of ever more polite but nonetheless still disqualifying theories of female political incapacity, both documented here, are precisely what one would expect to see if Pateman were correct. For a subtle but essentially sympathetic examination of Pateman's thesis, see Rachel Judith Weil, "Sexual Ideology and Political Propaganda in England, 1680–1714," Ph.D. thesis, Princeton University, 1991. (Ms. Weil is now in the Department of History, University of Georgia.) The process Pateman describes extends, then, from the essential masculinity of Lockean contract theory on through male appropriation of the enlightenment in general to the masculine possession of revolutionary thought depicted in Landes' *Women and the Public Sphere* and in Jan Lewis's "Motherhood and the Construction of the Male Citizen." This male appropriation of successive, potentially liberating ideologies in one sense provided the ground for continuing re-coalescences of intense misogyny and for male seizures of power; yet, as noted, neither Locke nor the enlightenment nor revolutionary ideology could be entirely appropriated by men, so that public misogyny, at heart, had to become more polite, and citizenship to some limited degree shared with women.

13. On the waning of "patriarchy" into "paternalism," again see Rhys Isaac, "Communication and Control" and Jay Fliegleman, *Prodigals and Pilgrims* (both sources in note 9, chapter 4, above); on the waning role of inheritance, see Daniel Scott Smith, " Parental Power and Marriage Patterns: An Analysis of Historical Trends in Hingham, Massachusetts," *Journal of Marriage and the Family*, 35 (August 1973), 419–28.

INDEX

INDEX

INDEX

INDEX